The Additional Michael Frayn

Michael Frayn

The Additional
Michael Frayn

Methuen

Published by Methuen 2000

1 3 5 7 9 10 8 6 4

This collection first published in 2000 by
Methuen Publishing Ltd
215 Vauxhall Bridge Road, London SW1V 1EJ

Copyright © Michael Frayn 2000

Michael Frayn has asserted his rights under the
Copyright, Designs and Patents Act, 1988, to be identified
as the author of this work.

Methuen Publishing Limited Reg. No. 3543167

A CIP catalogue record for this book
is available from the British Library

ISBN 0 413 74760 3

Typeset in Century by MATS, Southend-on-Sea, Essex
Printed and bound in Great Britain by
Cox & Wyman Ltd, Reading, Berkshire

The story so far . . .

The genealogy of this book, and its relationship with its cousin *The Original Michael Frayn*, are rather tangled. So here, for anyone who happens to be interested, is the family history.

It all began somewhere around the middle of the last century, when I used to write a newspaper column. Nowadays, of course, everyone writes newspaper columns. You write one yourself, and think nothing of it, but in those far-off days there were very few of us doing it, and the appearance of a column in the papers occasioned almost as much curiosity and mirth as the sight of a horseless carriage in the streets. Which was fortunate, if the column you wrote happened to be a humorous one, as mine was.

I wrote my column three times a week in the *Guardian*, from 1959 until 1962, and then once a week for six years in the *Observer*. Governments came and fell. Sex was invented. Novel intoxicants were tried. Things were protested against. Two hundred and thirty five of these columns were reprinted in four books that appeared at the time (*The Day of the Dog*, *The Book of Fub*, *On the Outskirts* and *At Bay in Gear Street*). The rest were put to good use lighting fires or wrapping fish-heads for the cat, and have not been heard of since.

Time went by, and the world continued on its way much as before, even though I had ceased to write the column. Then in 1983 James Fenton selected 55 of the 235 reprinted pieces, and added a further 19 that had appeared too late for inclusion in the original 4 volumes. These 74 pieces were published as *The Original Michael Frayn*. Three years later Martin Jarvis recorded a selection of 31 pieces, drawn from the original 4 volumes plus the extra 19, under the title *Jarvis's Frayn*, and it was broadcast as a series on BBC Radio 4.

Then in 1994 I slipped briefly back into my old ways, and for a few months I found myself, rather to my surprise, writing a column again. How this had happened I attempted to explain in the last of these 33 later columns (reprinted here as 'A Good Stopping Place'). The following year 32 of them were published by Methuen under the title *Speak After the Beep*, together with 3 which had appeared elsewhere ('Money Well Changed' in the *Spectator*, 'A Pleasure Shared' in the *Independent*, 'Welcome Aboard' in a pre-publication dummy of the *Independent on Sunday*) and one unpublished piece ('The Cogitations of the Earl of Each'). In 1996 they were recorded by Martin Jarvis and broadcast as a new series on BBC Radio 4.

The present volume contains all 36 pieces from *Speak After the Beep*, together with 'Brought to Book', which appeared in the *Guardian* in 1999. I've added my own selection of 19 of the old pieces that *weren't* included in *The Original* (9 of which were first published in the *Guardian* and 10 in the *Observer*).

Now read on . . .

Contents

Welcome aboard!

Hi! My name's Mike, and I'm your author today. Welcome aboard, and thank you for choosing to read me. It's a pleasure for me to write for you, and I shall be doing my best to make your trip with this article a happy one.

I have twenty paragraphs of in-article entertainment for you today, and I shall be starting the service of meaningful sentences just as soon as I've finished with all these introductory announcements. Thank you.

We've a slight delay, I'm afraid, in getting Paragraph 1 under way. This is because we missed our place in the queue at the beginning of the article, due to essential announcements. I'm now expecting Paragraph 1 to run immediately after Paragraph 6. I apologise to readers for any inconvenience this may cause. Please bear with me. Thank you.

Just to keep you up to date: Paragraph 5 has been cancelled, due to the non-arrival of Paragraph 4. Rest assured that I'm doing everything in my power to rectify the situation. Thank you.

No, hold on. That *was* Paragraph 4. With any luck we should be getting away round about Paragraph 7. We shall be routing through Paragraph 8, with onward connections to Paragraphs 9 to 24, just as soon as we've found Paragraph 6.

In the meantime you might like to have advance warning of delays between Paragraphs 14 and 19, due to major grammatical works which are expected to last until the summer of 1997.

1

This is a call for readers of delayed Paragraph 6. This paragraph is not now expected to depart until after Paragraph 18.

Still waiting for clearance on Paragraph 7. I think we all need a bit of a break here, so I'm going to come round serving free asterisks.

* * *

I know how frustrating all these delays and cancellations are, but bear with me. What I'm trying to do is to bring Paragraph 9 forward, and see if we can make a start with that. There are an awful lot of words here that have got to be organised into paragraphs, and an awful lot of paragraphs all trying to go somewhere. They can't all get there at once! So bear with me. Thank you.

This is a staff announcement. Will whoever has the words for Paragraph 9 please go to Paragraph 8 immediately.

Just to keep you in the picture: Paragraph 10 has been withdrawn after complaints by religious leaders. Last-minute talks are going on between management and staff to save Paragraph 11. Paragraph 12 is covered by the thirty-year rule. Paragraph 13 has failed to meet the standards laid down by the European Commission.

Still having trouble with Paragraph 9, I'm afraid. I've been badly let down by my suppliers. Bear with me. Please accept another round of complimentary asterisks.

* * *

Right, Paragraph 9! Here it is at last, and this is what it says: 'Paragraph 27 . . .' What? I don't believe this! They've given me the wrong paragraph! Bear with me just a little longer, will you?

Will readers of delayed Paragraph 6 please go immediately to Paragraph 13, and extinguish all hope, ready for immediate disappointment.

Yes, I know you've been waiting a long time! You think *I'm* enjoying this? Look, I'm on my own here – I've no staff! I'm trying to write this entire article single-handed! All right? Just bear with me, will you!

Correction to my previous announcement: Paragraph 3 *is* running. Paragraph 3 has come in! I've got Paragraph 3 right here! Anyone here still waiting for Paragraph 3 . . .? No? No one interested in Paragraph 3 . . .? Is there any wonder I can't get staff? Is it surprising that morale in the industry is so low?

Look, I've had cutbacks, just like everybody else! I've no paper to write on! I'm struggling with a lot of obsolete equipment! Sitting on a broken chair – writing at a desk with three legs . . .!

Hold on . . . Right – we're ready to go at long last!

I've now used up my maximum permitted space, however, so I shall be leaving you at this point. It only remains for me to say thank you for bearing with me today. I hope that next time you're bearing with anyone, you'll bear with me.

Fun with numbers

I'm on my way to the cash-dispenser, and I'm feeling rather pleased with myself, because for once I've remembered to do it before I go into a shop or get into a taxi and find I've no money to pay with.

What I'm also doing as I walk along the street is rehearsing my personal number inside my head, to make sure I can still remember it. 4273 . . . 4273 . . . Yes, OK, got it. I'm being a little over-anxious, perhaps, but I don't want any embarrassments of the sort I've had in the past, when I've put the card in the machine in front of a long queue of people, and got 'Incorrect personal number entered', and had to take it out again smartly before I also got 'Your card has been retained', then walk round the block for ten minutes while I calmed down and sorted out the digits in my mind. Not to mention the time when I put in the right number but the wrong card . . .

I won't think about that just now, though. I'll simply concentrate on the number. 4237 . . . 4237 . . . Right. Firmly in place. Everything's going to be all right.

It's just that it sounds a bit funny, somehow. 4327 . . . These machines are so pedantic – you not only have to have the right four digits, which you'd think would be enough to win you something reasonably substantial in the lottery, let alone get a few miserable pounds out of your own account, but you have to have them in the right order. Four digits in the right order! That must be worth at least ten thousand pounds of someone else's money!

But it's all right, because I have a mnemonic. One of

4

my daughters, who is a little shaky on numbers, taught me this trick. At one stage in her career she had to remember a four-digit number to get past security into her job every morning. She explained to me that, since literature was more her kind of thing than mathematics, she had turned the number into a story, about a young woman of 27 who was having an affair with a man of 54. I said I couldn't see how she remembered that it wasn't a woman of 24 having an affair with a man of 57, or for that matter a man of 31 and a woman of 62, and she said, no, nor could she, now I mentioned it. And a terrible uncertainty came into her voice.

My daughter is now self-employed. In any case I was never very convinced by this love affair. I find it difficult to remember my own age, let alone the ages of fictitious characters, because ages keep changing. My mnemonic is purely mathematical – a much more solid basis. Three of the digits in my number, as you can see, are an anagram of three naturally sequential digits, and the fourth digit is the sum of the last two digits in the sequence.

Actually this is a fictitious version of my mnemonic, because, needless to say, we're talking about a fictitious version of my personal number. If I published the real one, not only might you be tempted to hack into my account, but, much worse, the bank would insist on changing the number, as they did once before, when the cards and the numbers got themselves crossed, and then I should have to start remembering a new mnemonic.

Which would be a pity, because the real mnemonic I've got is so elegant. Let me just say, without giving too much away, that the *first* digit is *two* larger than the *third*, so I just remember one, two, three. Yes? Then the *fourth* digit is the sum of the *third* and the *second* – easy, because four is one more than three, and then we're simply going back down the scale again: four, three,

5

two . . . Hold on . . . What's the second digit? Yes, right, sorry – I'm getting confused – the *second* digit is two more than the first . . . Or twice as much as the first. . . . Or rather . . .

Anyway, I don't need to remember the mnemonic – I can always work out the mnemonic from the number. Except that while I was trying to remember the mnemonic the number's gone out of my head.

You'll notice how calm I'm keeping about this. No blind panic, as you might have expected, even though I've already walked past the machine while all this has been going on, and I'm going to have to go on and walk all the way round the block again while I get it sorted out. In fact it doesn't actually matter at all that I can't remember the number – just so long as I *remember* I can't remember it – because I've got it written down in this little electronic organiser thing I keep in my pocket here for exactly this kind of eventuality.

I'm not giving any secrets away here. The number isn't written in some place where you could find it even if you came round and stole my little organiser thing – or worse, my God, if someone checking up from the bank stole it! – but in a special bit you can't get into without entering a secret number. And yes, don't worry, I *can* remember this number, because with simple cunning it's my bank machine number written backwards . . .

Which of course in this particular case presents a problem. Or *would* present a problem, if I hadn't taken the precaution of writing down the secret number in the non-secret part of the organiser. And that's perfectly secure, because it's disguised as a telephone number. *You* don't know which of the thousand telephone numbers in the list it is, but *I* know it's the one that belongs to a fictitious character called. . . .

Well, the name will come back to me in a minute . . .

6

And if it doesn't, never mind, bit of a nuisance, but I've got this thing covered every way – I took the name out of a book lying on the third shelf up from the bottom in my office. I'll just have to go back to my office first. And don't think I'm not going to be able to get into my office – that in my rising panic I have forgotten the code to punch into the keypad on the door, because the code is very simply the date of one of the major battles in European history, with two of the digits transposed, and I may be able to forget a mnemonic, but I'm not likely to forget the name of a *battle* . . .

Except that I have.

No! This is not possible! This is pure self-sabotage! I'm talking myself into this!

Calm down. Think . . . Right, here's what I do. I jump into a cab and I go to a reference library and I look through some standard work on European history from, say, 1300 to 1900. Won't take all that long if I can just find a . . . and yes, there *is* one, my luck's changed! *Taxi* . . .! Take me to the local library, will you . . .?

No, sorry, hold on. Of course – I've no money on me. Take me to a cash machine . . . Oh, we're next to it . . . Wait – I'll be two minutes . . . As long as I can remember my number . . .

Ah. Yes. Right. Problem. And now there's a pound on the taxi meter. This is going to be embarrassing.

No, it's not. Let's go right back to the beginning. Back to the moment when I was walking towards the cash-dispenser, and I was remembering my personal number. Because I can remember remembering it. So it must be in my head somewhere.

Right, then, clear everything else out. Never mind remembering – concentrate on forgetting. Forget the taxi standing there. Forget the meter ticking away. Forget the traffic, forget the world. Forget the little organiser thing, forget the mnemonics. Just go down through the veils of consciousness into the deep, dark caverns of memory ... down to the lost golden hoard of codes and numbers ...

And I've got there!

Battle of Lepanto, 1571!

Right, here we go. One ... five ... seven ... one ... What's this? 'Incorrect personal number entered.' Of course – I didn't transpose the digits! Try again. One ... seven ... five ... one ... No, no, no! Five ... seven ... one ... one. ... Seven ... one ... one ... five ...

What? 'Your card has been retained ...' No! Stop! Come back! I made a mistake – that was the battle – that was the door! Listen – I've remembered the fictitious character! He's 84! He's having an affair with a woman called Rosemary ...!

Week Two

1 And on the morning of the eighth day God woke up, greatly refreshed by His rest. And He remembered His work, that He had finished on the sixth day, and that He had beheld, and that He had seen was very good.

2 And He looked at it again. And behold, it was not very good at all, it was very bad.

3 The winged fowl was flying above the earth in the open firmament of heaven, it was true, and the creeping thing was creeping upon the earth. But the creeping thing was creeping upon the earth in considerably fewer numbers than might have been expected, because, lo, the winged fowl was zooming down out of the firmament of heaven and eating the creeping thing.

4 Meanwhile the fowl of the air was getting eaten by the beast of the earth, and the beast of the earth was getting eaten by the fowl of the air, and some of the creeping things were creeping right off the earth, and installing themselves in various warm corners of the beasts and fowls, where *plainly* they had never been intended to be.

5 And He looked at man, and He got a worse shock still. He had granted man dominion over the fish of the sea, certainly – but dominion was one thing, and what man appeared to be doing to the fish population of the world's shallower seas was quite another. Nor could any reasonable person think that the concept of dominion was ever intended to include all the things that man was trying out on the fowl of the air and the cattle, which involved pieces of specially sharpened flint and captive bolt pis-

tols. All right, a little latitude in the case of the creeping things might possibly be allowed, since no one had much sympathy for them, and they were behaving in such a pestilential fashion themselves. But this could not for a moment be said about the great whales, which were extremely lovable, and almost human, and bothering no one at all apart from some tiny organisms which God could not even remember figuring in the original list.

6 It was strange. God remembered being immensely pleased with man when He had created him. He remembered the good feeling He had had at the end of the sixth day. Now He could not remember for the life of Him what He had been so pleased about. He began to think that He should have stopped much sooner, possibly on the first day, as soon as He had done the light, which was a brilliant success, everyone said so.

7 Though it would have been a terrible shame if He had stopped before He had done the grass, and the herb yielding seed, and the tree yielding fruit. These had all got wonderful reviews, and the only trouble was that they were succumbing fast before the depredations of His subsequent efforts.

8 Oh, and the fourth day had been one of the great days. At the time it had seemed no different from all the others, but looking back He couldn't think how He had ever done anything as simple and daring as the two great lights that ruled the day and night, and the stars also. He hadn't thought about them! He'd just done them! Now people were writing poems about them.

9 Though now apparently man was doing something rather nasty to one of the great lights, and getting extremely confused about the stars.

10 He felt rather like tearing the whole thing up and forgetting about it. Or perhaps if He redesigned some of the beasts a bit, and made them more herbivorous ...

10

Though then that would ruin the whole concept of the fruit and the herbs. It seemed crazy to throw away perfectly good fruit and herbs just to fix the problem with the lions and tigers.

11 And on the ninth day God began to get very depressed about how He had really been able to create things back then in the early days, when He had done the trees and the stars. Now, who knows, maybe He was finished. Maybe He would never be able to create anything ever again.

12 And God thought, It was taking that day off, that's when it all went wrong. I knew it was a mistake – I only did it because My Wife kept on about having a holiday. Though heaven knows, He *needed* a day off, He'd been working all the hours that He had made, for the entire week, and if you can't take an occasional day off then what's the *point* of it all?

13 Yes, now He came to think about it, what *was* the point of it all?

14 And God thought about how He should perhaps have created one of the other possible universes He had had in mind – for instance, the one that consisted of differently-shaped smells, or the one that was all in the subjunctive.

15 And on the ninth day God became so depressed about the whole thing that He showed it to His Wife, and asked Her what *She* thought. He couldn't really *see* it any more, He explained – He'd been living with it for nine days, He was too close to it. He would really value Her opinion.

16 And His Wife said it was wonderful, and that She liked it, She genuinely did – She wasn't just trying to reassure Him. She thought that He had done something absolutely *unique*. She really adored the beasts of the earth, especially the aardvark and the velociraptor.

17 And God said, yes, He quite liked the velociraptor, too. But how about the squid? She hadn't said anything about

the squid. He had been trying to do something rather special when He had made the squid.

18 And His wife said, yes, She liked the squid, the squid was a wonderful creation, particularly fried in batter. But there was something that worried Her just a tiny bit.

19 And God said, Oh? What was that?

20 And She said that it was only a small thing, and perhaps She shouldn't mention it.

21 But God said, No, go on, be absolutely frank, I never mind constructive criticism.

22 And His Wife said, Well, She wasn't absolutely sure about the chihuahua.

23 And God opened His eyes very wide in absolute amazement and said, You're not sure about the *chihuahua?*

24 And She said, Well, not absolutely. And just possibly, if She was being completely honest, there was also something a bit funny about the jellyfish.

25 Whereupon God grew extremely wrath. He would have understood, He said, if She had had doubts about the funnel-web spider or the staphylococcus or man. He had grave doubts about the last two Himself. But the chihuahua and the jellyfish just happened to be the two best things in the whole of creation, the only things that He was entirely happy with, and if She couldn't see that then She would never understand anything about His work at all.

26 And God's Wife flounced out of the room, and there was silence in heaven for about the space of half an hour.

27 And on the twelfth day His Wife came back and said She was sorry, She realised He was under tremendous pressure, and if He was really worried about man, why didn't He try creating woman as well? A woman might have some sort of moderating and civilising influence.

She might help man get more in touch with his feelings, and talk about things.

28 And God said that this was quite frankly the most ridiculous idea He had heard in all His born days, of which, He added, He had had more than She had had hot dinners.

29 And She said, Well, it was just an idea.

30 And on the thirteenth day God created woman. It smacked to Him of compromise, and He wasn't very happy about it, but He had to admit He couldn't really think of anything better. Anyway, in the end You had to make compromises here and there, You had to be prepared to learn from practice and listen to other people's points of view, He saw that.

31 And on the fourteenth day God won the *Yorkshire Post* Universe of the Year Award, and He made an acceptance speech that got a few laughs, and His Wife wore her dark blue silk with the pearl choker, and behold, things didn't seem quite so bad after all.

Making a name for yourself

Writing a novel, as any novelist will tell you, is hard. Writing a short story, as any short story writer will be eager to add, is harder still. The shorter the form the harder it gets. Poems are hell. Haiku are hell concentrated into seventeen syllables.

Until finally you get down to the shortest literary form of all, which is the title of whatever it is you're writing. Long-distance novelists who can happily write several thousand words a day for months on end then go into creative agonies when the time comes to compose the two or three words that will go on the spine. Battle-hardened samurai of the haiku take instruction from Zen masters before they attempt to extract an odd syllable out of their hard-won seventeen to go in the index.

This year, for various reasons, four different works of mine have reached the point where they need titles, and I've reached the point where I need hospitalisation. It's not that I can't write titles. I've written far more titles than anything else in my life. For one of these four projects I have 107 titles. For another – 74. For the third – 134. 134 titles! For one short book! 134 pretty good titles, though I say so myself. The trouble is you don't want 134 pretty good titles. You want one perfect title.

No titles at all so far for the fourth project, but this is because I haven't written the thing yet. Though after the agonies I've had with the other three I'm starting to wonder if I shouldn't write the title of this one first, then dash down a few thousand words to fit it.

The curious thing is that you usually do have a title first. You have the working title, that you put on the front of the file when you begin work, just so that you know which file's which. The working title, as its name suggests, works. That's to say, it actually succeeds in telling you which file's which, and it does it without being pretentious, or facetious, or unintentionally obscene. But the publisher, or the producer, or whoever it is, doesn't like it. Your agent doesn't like it – your partner doesn't like it. No one likes it. This may be because they don't know about it – you haven't told them. You know you can't use the working title. Life has to be harder than that.

One of the troubles with a list of 134 titles is that it offers odds of at least 133 to 1 against getting it right. I've got it wrong many times in the past. There's only one novel of mine that anyone ever remembers – and for all practical purposes it's called *The One About Fleet Street*, because even the people who remember the book can't remember the title I gave it. I wrote another book called *Constructions*. I think I realised even before publication that I'd picked a dud here, when my own agent referred to it in the course of the same conversation once as *Conceptions* and once as *Contractions*.

I suppose it must be even worse being ennobled, and having to find a title to give yourself. *You're* not going to go out of print and be pulped. You're going to be stuck with being Lord Conceptions, or Baroness Contractions, for the rest of your life. The thought of the torments that new peers must go through makes me look at the House of Lords with a fresh respect.

As with a book, of course, you start with a perfectly good little working title. When the Prime Minister's office writes with the good news you're G. E. Bodd, of The Moorings, Oakdene Avenue, Carshalton Beeches. You

15

could perfectly well become Lord Bodd of somewhere. Lord Bodd of Carshalton, why not? Lord Bodd of The Moorings? Or Lord Moorings of the Beeches, perhaps? You never consider any of them for a moment. You'd be ashamed to mention them to the College of Arms.

You let your imagination take flight a little. You want something that celebrates the rise of the Bodds of Carshalton with some suitable panache – something that brings a touch of good old-fashioned romance to the world – something that your friends can remember. Lord Mountfitchet of Compton Pauncefoot? The future Lady Mountfitchet doesn't like it. Lord Lafite-Rothschild of Sampford Peverell? Too many syllables, says Garter King of Arms – toastmasters will never be able to say it. So how about something nice and Scottish? That always sounds attractively baronial. Lord McDrumlin of Dundreggan? Rouge Dragon says there's a superstition in the business that Scottish titles bring bad luck.

You play with the idea of something extravagantly modest and self-deprecating. Lord Dymm of Dull. Lord Little of Mere. But Rouge Croix says that in the highly competitive peerage of today you are liable to be overlooked if you don't sell yourself hard. You go to the opposite extreme. For the whole of one afternoon you have absolutely decided that you will be Lord Magnificence of Belgravia. One of the Pursuivants – Portcullis, probably – says this is too abstract. You wake up in the middle of the night knowing with absolute conviction that you want to be Lord Lashings of Styal. Portcullis quite likes it, but it doesn't really speak to Bluemantle.

You decide to forget grandeur, and be entirely up-to-date and straightforwardly commercial. You flirt with Lord Brookside of Coronation Street. Then you think, no, if we're going down into the marketplace, let's get right down there and quite frankly sell ourselves. You submit

16

a shortlist to the Heralds that includes Lord Knight of Passion and Lord Stirrings of Lust. There is no reply from the Heralds.

You'd really like to find something absolutely plain and straightforward that reflected your character in some way. Lord Baggs of Enthusiasm, perhaps? The Heralds say there is already a Lord Baggs of Foulness. Then you go through a whimsical phase, when you fancy spending the rest of your life as Lord Much of Amuchness. The Chester Herald *loves* it, but the Windsor Herald can't find Amuchness, even on the large-scale Ordnance Survey. He can find Sale and Hay, it's true, but there's already a Lord Conditions and the Lancaster Herald for some reason hates Lord Bundles. You feel that Lord Fax of Uckfield has a certain ring, or alternatively Lord Hunt of Cuckfield. The Heralds turn them both down. They will not explain why.

By the time you have gone through 134 permutations you are ready to grasp at anything. Anything! Yes, why not? Lord Anything of Interest. Lord Anything of Anywhere . . .

In the end you go back to your working title. Lord Bodd. It has the advantage of saying what it means. Bodd is who you are, after all. You still jib at Carshalton, though. Then you remember you have a great-aunt living in Budleigh Salterton. At the eleventh hour you settle blindly for your 135th effort – Lord Bodd of Budleigh. As soon as you've sent it in you realise it's a disaster, but it's too late for 136th thoughts.

No one's going to remember, anyway. The first time you go to the House, Lord Doss of Liss introduces you to Lord Loss of Diss as Lord Budd of Dudley, whereupon Lord Loss of Diss introduces you to Lord Ladd of Lydd as Lord Dudd of Didley.

And what most people are going to call you is Lord

What's He Called, the One Who Used To Be What Was
His Name, Only He Got the Sack.

Please be seated

Breakfast in bed – there's nothing like it! Nothing like it for making you realise what wonderful inventions the table and chair are.

The position forced upon you by having breakfast in bed is a torment in itself. Making prisoners sit up with their legs straight out in front of them and their back unsupported is (I hope) outlawed under United Nations conventions on torture. But now here you are, not detained without charge in the jails of a Third World dictatorship, but on a well-earned holiday in a rather expensive hotel covered by the protocols of the European Community, and your wife has said that she would like breakfast in bed, so the humanitarian efforts of the United Nations do not apply.

But, as the meal proceeds, your position deteriorates still further. You have of course been eating with extreme circumspection so as not to get toast-crumbs into the bed. You have stomach-cramp from leaning forwards over the tray, and in fact you haven't even touched the toast, because you're not such a fool as to think you can eat toast in bed in any way at all, even with a bag over your head, without getting the crumbs into the bed with you. You have eaten nothing so far but the grapefruit – and you haven't even eaten the grapefruit, because trying to prise the segments free shook the tray, and made the coffeepot rock wildly from side to side. In spite of all this care, however, crumbs have mysteriously begun to break off the toast of their own accord, and creep surrep-

19

titiously off the tray and down into the sheets. These toast-crumbs, by the feel of it, are now enjoying breakfast in bed themselves. The breakfast they are enjoying is you.

With extreme circumspection, since you have this complex array of uneaten toast and brimming hot liquids balanced across your knees, you shift your bottom away from the crumbs. So now you are no longer quite sitting up. You are sustaining yourself at a slight angle to the vertical, in even more flagrant contravention of international law. Gradually the angle increases, and you begin to slide down the bed. The strain becomes unbearable. But, since you don't wish to share the bed with half-a-litre of scalding coffee as well as the toast-crumbs, you do not make any of the sudden or convulsive movements that you long to make. You put your hands on the bed and gently... gently... ease yourself... together with the tray on top of you... into a better position.

But now you realise with dismay that the butter and marmalade which have somehow got on your fingers, in spite of your never having touched them, have transferred themselves to the sheets. The entire bed is becoming a toast and marmalade sandwich. You look for the napkin to clean things up. It has withdrawn in a cowardly manner to the relative safety of the floor. You lean with infinite precaution sideways over the edge of the bed to reach it... The napkin seems be withdrawing still further as your fingers approach. For one brief moment you take your eye off the tray to see what's going on... And at that moment the tray moves quietly and decisively out of the horizontal.

I see why bed-bugs like having breakfast in bed. Why women do I find rather more obscure.

It scarcely bears thinking about, but there must have been a time, before civilisation began, when people had to have breakfast in bed every morning, because there wasn't anywhere else to have it – neither the table nor the chair had yet been invented. In fact people must have had lunch in bed as well. And tea, and dinner. In fact, sitting, in the sense that we know it, with knees bent, and feet stored on a lower level, had not been discovered! Apart from sitting up in a right-angle with a tray across your knees, there were only two known positions that the human body could take up – vertical and horizontal. The only alternative to sitting up in bed to eat was to do it lying down, and choking to death. Or else to go to someone's party, and eat standing up.

This last alternative was so awful that it's almost certainly what inspired the crucial advance to the table and chair. Archaeologists believe that it occurred during the Sumerian civilisation, some time after the invention of the wheel, around 2100 BC. King Ur-Nammu, the founder of the third dynasty of Ur, is thought to have held a particularly important banquet at about this time, where the guests would have been required to remain vertical all the way from cocktails at 7.00 p.m. until the brandy and cigars, somewhere around midnight.

For five hours they would have been holding massive gold plates, with huge silver goblets of wine clipped to them by the newly-invented wineglass-holder (in lightweight plastic, it's true, but encrusted with large uncut chalcedonies), transferring the knife from the right hand to the left after cutting up each mouthful of meat, and simultaneously transferring the fork from the left to the right in order to eat it, then transferring the entire plate from one hand to the other before the wrist finally gave way under the strain, and in so doing dropping the knife or the fork, or both, and then, in recovering the knife and fork, tipping gravy down the front of some great court official's shirt, then searching for the napkin to wipe him down, and finding it . . . not on the floor, where you would expect a napkin to be, but clenched underneath the plate in fingers which had by now become so paralysed that the napkin could not be prised free without dropping the plate.

Alcohol had already been invented, specifically in order to offer some hope of escape from this situation into the horizontal and the unconscious. But how to get at the alcohol with one's hands tied up like this?

And then, somewhere around midnight at this particular banquet, it is believed, Ur-Nammu himself suddenly buckled at the knees. By chance he was standing in front of the radiogram (as the audio system was then called). The sound of Carroll Gibbons and his Savoy Orpheans ended in a noise like a sword ripping through chainmail, and in the terrible silence that followed everyone looked round to see that the king was no longer vertical.

But then neither was he horizontal. He was caught in a curious position halfway between the two, his bottom resting on the radiogram, folded at the waist and again at the knees, so that he formed a kind of zigzag. It was a profoundly comic sight, but no one dared to laugh. Then Ur-Nammu smiled. 'This is delightful,' he said, so far as can be made out from the hieroglyphs in the society columns next morning. 'It is a huge advance upon standing up. I shall call this *sitting down*.'

Sitting down became all the rage. Everyone in Ur, Kish, Ahkshak, Hamazi, and the other cities of Mesopotamia sat. Some sat on record-players or television-sets, some (agonisingly) on radiators, some on ashtrays and umbrella stands, some on discarded sandwiches. Very soon the first purpose-built *chairs* began to appear (though of course their full potential couldn't be realised until the invention of leaning back). It may be a coinci-

22

dence, but life-expectancy in the Sumerian world rose by forty-seven per cent about this time.

Life was still not perfect. People still had to balance their plates on their knees, together with glasses of red and white wine and Perrier water, plus napkin, cutlery, side-plates, crackers, balloons, going-home presents, and the text of any speeches which they proposed to make, and there were some who found this difficult. Another thirty years elapsed before Ur-Nammu's successor Amar-Su'en made the next great advance. He was still a student at the time, and although he was himself sitting on a specialised development of the chair called a throne, a lot of his fellow-students were sprawling about on the floor, as students will. Among them was a delightful girl reading Social Sciences and Early Hittite, who was sitting literally at his feet, and laughing in a most satisfactory way at all his jokes. She was saying quite amusing things herself, too, and Amar-Su'en was suddenly taken with the desire to slap his thighs to demonstrate his appreciation. So, to clear his thighs for slapping, he had the idea of balancing his plate on her head.

After that he took the girl to all the parties he went to, and grew so attached to her that he stood everything on her head, from vases of flowers to typewriters. When she subsequently died of pressure on the brain he was heartbroken. But the custom spread, until political developments began to make it increasingly difficult to find volunteers for the task. Soon cheap substitutes made of marble or carved mahogany took their place – and the table as we know it today took shape.

At last the human race was getting somewhere. Nouvelle cuisine and quantum theory followed in short order. So let us give thanks for the table and chair – and please, *please*, let us make full use of them.

That having been said

I've been visiting the local Old Tropes Home.

I'm very concerned about what happens to expressions and metaphors in their old age. They start out in life so fresh and colourful, so full of humour, so eager to please. They're worked day in and day out over the years until they're exhausted – then they're brutally shoved to one side to make room for younger and more energetic expressions. I believe that they shouldn't have to eke out their last few years of life on the streets, taking any work they can get, spurned and abused. They should be looked after among their own kind in quiet and dignified surroundings.

In the place I've found the residents were obviously made very comfortable. Comfortable with and about everything, even the most appalling ideas and decisions. In fact they seemed particularly comfortable about Attila the Hun. There was a statue of him, placed somewhat to the left of the building, so that almost everything inside was somewhat to the right of him.

The Matron who showed me round spoke very reassuringly. 'I understand where you're coming from,' she said. 'So let me just bring you up to speed. We're very definitely state of the art here, and I don't need to tell you which art that is – it's the art of living. And if you're up at the sharp end then you've got to get your act together and show your street cred. That having been said, what gets up my nose is that people can't get their heads around this. I mean, what are we talking?'

I said it sounded to me like some dialect of English.

'We're talking serious money,' she said. 'We're talking megabucks. Because what are we looking at here?'

So far as I could see it seemed to be the ancient flagpole outside the window, up which things were run to see if anyone saluted them.

'We're looking at ten grand a day,' she said. 'Ten K – and I do mean K. Because, make no mistake, the sky's the limit. That said, you pays your money and you takes your pick.'

The social range of the residents was wide. As she showed me round the Matron pointed out both the Poor Man, to whom many things here were said to belong, curiously enough, and the Thinking Man, who apparently owned much of the rest. But everyone there seemed to be terribly good value. Indeed, they were all getting increasingly better value. Because things in the Home don't just get increasingly whatever, or more whatever. They get increasingly more whatever it is. There seems to be an acceleration involved here which bears the fingerprints of the pace of modern living.

Some of the residents were in poor shape. Things had cost them an arm and a leg – often as a result of prices going through the roof, and the roof falling in, so that the bottom had dropped out of the market. Some of them looked as if they'd had a coach and horses driven through them.

A very decrepit old trope called Arguably buttonholed me in the corridor. 'In the last twenty years or so,' he told me, 'I have become arguably the most common word in the English language. I have arguably been responsible for making more unconfirmed statements possible than ever before in human history, and I've arguably saved writers and speakers more mental effort than the word processor and the dictating machine combined.'

He thought for a little, though not very hard.

'Then again,' he said, 'equally arguably I haven't.'

Couples are not separated in the Home. You can see them wandering along the corridors together, hand in hand, touchingly devoted. This Day and Age – they're still as much in love as ever. If you see First you're bound to see Foremost. Sick and Tired were being wheeled along in a double bathchair by Hale and Hearty. Care and Attention were being utterly devoted to all the Hopes and Fears. Though one Fear had left the family group and gone off with Trepidation. Now they've grown so alike that a lot of people can't tell them apart.

The old tropes are a remarkably lively lot, considering. 'We *have sex* a great deal,' one of them told me. I expressed surprise. 'Oh,' he said, 'we have it pretty well non-stop. Look through this keyhole. You see? People having every single variant of sex listed in the OED! Everything from (1) *either of the two divisions of organic beings distinguished as male and female respectively*, through to (2) *quality in respect of being male or female* – even (3) *the distinction between male and female in general*'!

My informant thumbed through a greasy copy of the OED. 'It doesn't stop there, either,' he whispered hoarsely. 'The OED says that this third usage is now often associated with a *more explicit notion*.' He licked his lips and bent closer towards me as he read it out. '*The sum of those differences in the structure and function of the reproductive organs on the grounds of which beings are distinguished as male and female, and of the other physiological differences consequent on these*.'

These torrid relationships and steamy romances raise the temperature and humidity of the Home so that everyone gets a little hot under the collar. The clouds of vapour given off by all this may be the mysterious *yonks* which so many people haven't seen each other for.

To take the inmates' minds off sex there is a playing-field attached to the Home, and great efforts are made to ensure that it is a level one – though people are apparently always moving the goal-posts. Efforts to organise a piss-up in the local brewery have not yet been successful. The local vicar sometimes invites inmates to the original vicarage tea-party. No one ever goes, though, because everything in the Home has been made to look like it already, even the steamiest sessions of distinction between male and female.

In the dining-room residents were making a meal of it – and that was just for starters. Some of the dishes on the menu were out of this world. In fact they were to die for, and if they weren't to die for they were the kind of thing you'd kill to get your hands on. So, one way or another, by the end of meals a fair number of the residents tend to be out of this world as well.

In other words, they'd had their chips, which was just as well, because when the chips are down there's no such thing as a free lunch. It's not a picnic here, after all – naturally enough, since some of the inhabitants are two sandwiches short of one. In the circumstances I was not surprised to be told that most of them were quite frankly out to lunch.

The Home is organised along military lines. I talked to inmates who were proud to belong to the Gin and Tonic Brigade and the Blue Rinse Brigade. The Green Welly Brigade have a reputation for profligacy with the brigade colours – they are always giving things a bit of welly.

I could hear the most alarming noises of protest in the background, but the Matron explained that this was coming from the twentieth century, into which various things were being dragged kicking and screaming, entirely for their own benefit.

I asked why some of the residents were being made to stand in silence with their faces to the wall. The Matron said that they were members of the chattering classes – people who had had the temerity to talk about politics and other public matters that concerned them. She also pointed out a group of luvvies – actors and actresses who had ludicrously attempted to vary their slothful round of unemployment and awards ceremonies with some kind of pretence at seriousness. They were being put down hard and sent up rotten.

In some of the rooms there was scarcely room to swing a cat – though this was impossible to check because, as the Matron explained, the cat was in hell, and it didn't have much chance of surviving. About as much as a snowball, she thought. Though, if the snowball managed to survive until hell froze over it would find itself in a whole new ballgame.

They did have a handcart for going to hell in, said the Matron, if I wanted to go down that particular road, and she wished me the best of British. But before we could get the ball rolling all hell broke loose.

An inmate in bell-bottomed trousers staggered up and flung his money around. He was not, he explained, flinging his money around like a drunken sailor – he *was* the drunken sailor like whom everybody else flung their money around. Very difficult to know, in that case, I suggested, how he himself was flinging his money around. Was it, I asked, like money was going out of fashion? Not at all, he replied, it was like there was no tomorrow.

It was plainly crunch time, and the Matron cracked down hard, though she papered over the cracks as best she could. But no way could the crackdown be made to bite unless it was given teeth.

As I left I met a new arrival, still looking relatively fresh-faced. 'Political Correctness,' he introduced himself. 'I feel I'm a bit past my sell-by date. And since the whole idea of a sell-by date has gone down the tubes itself some time ago, like the tubes it went down, I thought I'd join it in here, and we could all pop our clogs together.'

Because that said, what's it all about, at the end of the day? What's the bottom line? Let me spell it out to you in words of one syllable – the bottom line is this.

I say Toronto, you say Topeka

Flying, I gather, is not such a high-stress occupation as it used to be, because the stress is being shifted from the aircrew on to computers. But it's increasingly a wrong-stress occupation, as the stress is shifted off the significant word in cabin announcements on to the auxiliary verb.

It used to be just on American airlines. But now even British cabin staff are telling us that the plane *will* be landing shortly at London Heathrow. Passengers *will* be disembarking from the front of the aircraft, they insist. We *are* requested to make sure we have all our belongings with us.

I used to think this was because airlines were hiring actors or theatre directors to coach their cabin crew in diction. Actors and directors who perform the classics *have* to find new ways of stressing the lines, to stop themselves going crazy. Or rather, they have to *find* new ways, they have to find new *ways*, new ways of *stressing*, of stressing the *lines*. They are acutely aware that this is not the first time in history that someone has gone on to a stage and said, 'Oh what a rogue and peasant slave am *I*!' They know that at least twenty-seven other actors are going to be saying it somewhere in the world at that very same moment. Their soul revolts! 'Oh, *what* a *rogue*!' they find themselves gurgling. And a new reading of the part – the prince as queen – has come into being even before they're halfway through the line.

Some actors I've worked with can effortlessly hit every

stress in a line except the right one. I am overcome by stress-blindness myself, reading my own plays through to directors. I can't remember for the life of me what stress I had in mind when I wrote the line. All I know is that it's certainly not the *one* I'm managing to produce.

But now another explanation altogether has come to me. We're surprised to be told that the cabin staff *will* be serving lunch because we were taking it for granted that they would be. But maybe we were taking it entirely too much for granted. Maybe the serving of lunch is no more pre-ordained than anything else in life. Cabin staff are human beings, not automata. They are free citizens, not slaves. They have ideas of their own about whether lunch should be served or not – and a tremendous debate has probably been going on about it in the galley ever since take-off. 'We *won't* serve lunch!' say some of the attendants. 'We *may*, in certain circumstances,' say others. 'We *could* . . . we *should* . . . we *must*' – the argument rages. The passengers ought to be asking each other: 'Will they, or won't they?' They should be taking bets on the outcome. So that when the Chief Stewardess comes out of the negotiating chamber and goes on the air to announce 'We *will* be!' she is issuing hot news. We should all cheer.

Evidently the same kind of thing is going on up there in the cockpit. A battle royal has been raging about the flight-plan, ever since the Chief Stewardess predicted confidently, shortly before take-off: 'We *will* be departing for Cincinnati.' This was in line with well-informed forecasts by both the airline and air-traffic control. But now, up there in the cockpit, the Captain has suddenly raised the possibility of flying to somewhere else altogether.

'I favour Decatur, Illinois,' he tells the First Officer. 'I've heard good things of Decatur.'

The First Officer, a man of little imagination and rigid

principles, is frankly astonished. 'I don't understand,' he says. 'We're cleared through to Cincinnati.'

'I don't much care for Cincinnati,' says the Captain.

'But this is Flight JQ407,' says the First Officer. 'For Cincinnati.'

'As I understand it from Operation Control,' says the Captain, 'Flight JQ407 went to Cincinnati yesterday.'

'Exactly!' says the First Officer.

'I believe it also went to Cincinnati the day before yesterday,' says the Captain, 'and the day before that.'

'It goes to Cincinnati every day,' says the First Officer.

'Then it has gone to Cincinnati often enough,' says the Captain. 'The possibilities of flying to Cincinnati have been very adequately explored. We have had Cincinnati.'

'But we are *contractually* bound to go to Cincinnati!' cries the First Officer, who read jurisprudence at North-Western before he went to air college. 'The front office sold the passengers their tickets on the basis of an *implied undertaking* to go to Cincinnati!'

These powerful stresses have no effect upon the Captain, because captains don't normally stress any words at all. When they talk to the passengers, as you may have noticed, they remain notably laid-back and unemphatic. And this particular captain happens to have read moral philosophy at UCLA.

'We also have a duty to ourselves,' he explains calmly, 'to realise our true potential, to behave with spontaneity and authenticity. I don't think that can best be done by going to Cincinnati.'

For some reason this catches the imagination of the Flight Engineer. 'It's not just *us*!' he cries, with hitherto unsuspected passion, and a wild storm of emphases. 'It's all those poor grey *passengers* back there! Let's bring a little colour into *their* lives! A little of the romance of the *unknown*! Some faint echo of the days of the great *clip-*

pers, when you were at the mercy of the four winds of *heaven*, and you never knew for sure which *continent* you were going to end *up* in!'

No one pays any attention to him. Too many stresses, possibly.

'We don't even know if there's an *airport* at Decatur!' says the First Officer.

'OK,' says the Captain, 'so here's what we do. We go down to treetop height and bop around for a bit, see what we can see. There may be a field. There may be a freeway where things are reasonably quiet.'

'I've got *another* idea!' says the Flight Engineer. 'There's this *girl* I know in Cedar Rapids, Iowa . . .'

'Well, *I* say we're going to Cincinnati!' shouts the First Officer.

'I say we're *not*,' says the Captain, finally driven to emphasising words himself. 'And *I* am the Captain.'

'You *are* the Captain, right!' says the First Officer, by which he means that *if* the Captain is the Captain then he should *behave* like the Captain.

But the Captain misses this implication. They didn't do rhetoric at UCLA.

'I *am* the Captain?' he says. 'OK, if that's the way you prefer it – I *am* the Captain. No, hold on, I was right the first time: I am the *Captain*. Is that what I said? You're getting me a little confused here.'

'What do you mean, *I'm* getting *you* confused?' screams the First Officer.

'No? OK. You're getting me *confused* . . . You're *getting* me confused . . . It sounds funny whichever way. It's these damned stresses! I am *the* Captain . . . I have a feeling that language is becoming meaningless. I don't know where I am, or what I'm doing. It's all like a dream . . .'

You probably noticed that the cabin staff didn't serve lunch immediately, in spite of having been so very insistent that they were going to. That's because they were all in the cockpit, tying up the Captain. And that supposed turbulence, somewhere over Altoona? That's when they were disarming the First Officer, and trying to resuscitate the Flight Engineer.

Don't worry – the plane is being flown by a very level-headed stewardess who saw a film once where this kind of thing happened. But clearly a firm statement had to be issued before rumours began to circulate back in the cabin. Well, you heard what the Chief Stewardess said: 'We *will* shortly be landing in Cincinnati!'

It was Churchillian.

Though when she added: 'We *hope* you've enjoyed flying with us,' I thought I detected the faintest note of doubt.

The long and the short of it

British Telecom, out of the goodness of their hearts, are running a major advertising campaign to persuade men to be more communicative. We don't talk for long enough on the phone, this is our problem, apparently. We compare unfavourably, in BT's view, with women, who are quite likely to sit down for chats with each other lasting half an hour at a time. BT approve of these 'simple joys'. They are pained by men's propensity to be 'short, sharp and to the point'.

A characteristic man's telephone conversation, they say, runs like this: 'Meet you down the pub, all right? See you there.' They find this 'abrupt'. I find it distinctly garrulous. 'Meet you there . . . see you there' – the poor fellow's saying everything twice. He also appears to be arranging to exchange a lot more conversation. Curious that this doesn't elicit BT's approval. Perhaps its beneficial spiritual qualities will be more appreciated by the brewers.

I can't imagine my friend W rambling on like this. BT would be even more deeply pained by *his* telephone calls – they're almost subliminally short. This has never been a problem between us, so far as I know. Quite the contrary. We have been good friends for thirty-seven years now, and in all that time we've never had a cross word. There wasn't a chance. The receivers were back on their rests before either of us had had an instant to check whether we had any grievances outstanding.

The last call I had from him was entirely character-

35

istic. He announced his name and asked me for a telephone number he needed. I told him the number. He said thank you, and put the phone down.

I have run through it again from memory, stopwatch in hand, and it lasted for approximately thirteen seconds. Thirteen seconds of pure communication – it seems to me to come close to the ideal. He could have left out telling me who he was, now I come to think about it, since I know that, and the 'thank you' was a rather time-consuming concession to convention. I suppose we could have got it down to about seven seconds, with a little more ruthlessness. But in an imperfect world thirteen seconds is not bad.

I can claim little of the credit for this exemplary brevity. The determining factor is W's iron self-discipline. Note, in the conversation recorded above, that he did not begin, as a less self-controlled person might have done, by asking if I was well. Nor did he finish up by doing it. A lot of people manage to stay off the subject until the last moment of a call, when their nerve suddenly goes. 'Oh, and how are you, by the way?' they say, with a concern so belated as to be insulting.

What you can't see, in the transcript above, is that W left no pause, either, between his courteous 'thank you' and his putting the phone down, for *me* to weaken, as I might well have done otherwise, not having his character and determination, and enquire after *his* health. 'Are you well?' I should have said, if there had been a finger's width of opportunity to say it in, in spite of not having the faintest desire for a medical bulletin. Why should I suddenly want to know how he was? He's been well for thirty-seven years now – and even if by some remote chance he'd suddenly stopped being well he wouldn't have dreamt of telling me.

'*Very* well,' he would have had to reply – simultaneously, for all I should have known at my end of the phone, trying to apply a tourniquet to a severed artery. Only four or five more seconds lost, it's true – but once we'd got this far politeness would have required him to add at least two more syllables. 'And you?' he would have had to enquire. 'Fine,' I should have been obliged to inform him, for all he knew with only my mouth still functioning among the bandages.

One more word from him – 'Good' – and we could have got back to what was left of our lives. But by this stage it would have been difficult for him to put the receiver down without an infinitesimal pause to see if I was proposing to say anything else. I *shouldn't* have been proposing to utter another word, of course. But now that this small hole had opened up in the fabric of the universe I should have felt compelled to fill it. I should have found myself telling him that it was very nice to hear from him. Before either of us knew what was happening I should have been enquiring after his wife and children, and various mutual friends. I should have forgotten the names of some of the people I was enquiring after, and should have had to filibuster in the hope of recalling them, or at any rate of making up for my apparent lack of concern in forgetting their names by the sheer amount of time I devoted to discussing them.

Somewhere around this point I should have remembered that we hadn't seen each other for some time. He would have felt obliged to suggest that we must bring this state of affairs to an end. We might even have got out our diaries, and negotiated vaguely back and forth over various more or less unsuitable dates in an indeterminate number of the weeks to come.

By now it would be dimly coming back to me that there *was* actually something of importance that I'd been

37

meaning to tell him. So then I should have had to keep the conversation going until I'd remembered what it was.

It's even within the bounds of possibility that I should have asked him what the weather was like at his end. Admittedly he was not phoning from another country, when mutual enquiries about the weather are required by international law. But he *was* on the other side of London. It's not particularly surprising if the weather's different in Australia, but it would be worthy of note if some completely different weather system had moved in on another Inner London borough.

Now that the conversation had acquired this much momentum, bringing it to an end would have been as difficult as halting a fully-laden container vessel. Eventually, however, driven by growing hunger if nothing else, one or the other of us would have had to make preliminary moves towards coaxing the great craft into its moorings. 'Well,' my friend might have said, 'I must get back to work.' And in the slight regretful pause that would naturally have followed this I should have heard myself asking: 'What are you working on at the moment?'

He would have told me. Very succinctly, of course, given his character – so succinctly that I should have had to pose a number of polite supplementaries.

Whereupon he would have had to ask me what *I* was working on. I should have given him a brief outline. As I did so I should have found myself warming to my theme. I should have begun to recall various small professional triumphs which had been insufficiently appreciated elsewhere, various major professional injustices to which I had been subjected, and for which I had not yet had sufficient sympathy.

I should have told him how difficult my life seemed to have become these days – how little time there was to get anything done. He would have told me how little time

38

he had. By now everyone but us would have left their workplaces and gone away to the country for the weekend, so it would have been too late for him to make the telephone call he had originally wanted the number for.

By now, in any case, night would have fallen. In the darkness, the scrap of paper on which he had noted down the number would have got brushed off his desk, and have disappeared behind some piece of furniture. He would not have instituted any search for it, because by this time he would have forgotten that he had ever wanted it.

As the dawn came up we should have told each other how nice it had been talking to each other. We should have asked each other to give our respective love to wives, children, aunts, neighbours. Just after he had finally managed to put the phone down I should have remembered what it was I had been meaning to tell him.

Crucial pieces of work now having been ruined on both sides, our respective careers would have languished, and we should both have fallen upon hard times. Since neither of us would have known about the other's plight, each of us would have been too proud to reveal his own, so we should never have rung each other again. Our thirty-seven years of friendship would have come to an end.

Thinking gratefully about how my friend's firmness of character had saved us from all this, I rang one of my daughters on some small point of information, and while I was about it I asked her for all her news, and she told me, and she asked me for mine, and I told her. In fact we gossiped away for the best part of an hour. British Telecom thought it was wonderful.

So did I, curiously enough.

Your quick flip guide

The quickest and flippest guide to all the
entertainment of history since the dawn of time!
Glance at it here and thank God you missed it!

10,000 million BC	**The Big Bang**. Would you believe a more mindless way of opening the schedules than *The Big Breakfast*? They must be desperate.
600,000 BC	**The Old Stone Age**. Carry On Chipping. And on. And on.
40,000 BC	**The *New* Stone Age**. It says here. You could have fooled us.
2500 BC	**The Pyramids**. Early undertakers' bills were shockers, too.
1220 BC	**The Ten Commandments**. They make 'em, you break 'em.
1200 BC	**The Holy Bible**. Something Old – something New – something borrowed – can it be true? Some enjoyably naff special effects, though, particularly with corpses coming back to life.
30 BC	**The Roman Empire**. Lashings of nosh and booze, and some great sex, if you don't mind sitting through all those battles first. Lions *v.* Christians makes a change from the UEFA Cup. (Some scenes may upset animal-lovers.)
AD **400**	**The Dark Ages**. Just when you thought it was safe to wake up and take an

interest again.

1066   **The Norman Conquest**. Ever wondered why so many of the nobs seem to have Frog names? No? Back to sleep again, then.

1337   **The Hundred Years War**. Creaking slasher featuring ex-pats *v.* colourful locals in well-loved holiday landscapes. And you thought *A Year in Provence* was long!

1347   **The Black Death**. Noir-ish but predictable medical nasty with rats and pustules.

1400   **The Renaissance**. The Italians may have lost at home to Croatia, but they invented art, wouldn't you know it?

1478   **The Spanish Inquisition**. Your one-stop action sudser – cops *and* firemen. Only here's the gizmo – the cops are all in drag and the firemen start the fires.

1508   **The Sistine Chapel**. Geniuses – who needs 'em? Fellow here who's *right* up the wall, not to mention across the ceiling. But watch out for God getting static electricity out of Melvyn Bragg.

1545   **The Council of Trent**. Predictable ecclesiastical romp. Could this be the original vicarage tea-party?

1564   **William Shakespeare**. So – whodunnit? Was it Will in the study with the quill? Or was it Francis in the back-parlour with the bacon? Or was it the butler all the time, and who cares?

1600   **The British Empire**. Stiff upper lip, chaps. The natives are restive – and they still haven't invented air-conditioning. (Black and white.)

1618 **The Thirty Years War**. Another leisurely ramble round the usual trouble-spots.

1687 **The Law of Gravitation**. When apples keep falling mysteriously off the apple trees, people suspect a poltergeist is at work. But eccentric scientist Isaac Newton believes there may be a more rational explanation . . .

PICK OF THE PICK

1739 **The War of Jenkin's Ear**. A real find. A fast-paced little war made on a shoestring, with a totally fresh and original starting point, that had a big influence in its time on better-known productions such as the War of the Austrian Succession. Terrific performance by Jenkin himself as the gung-ho mariner, and the severed ear is genuinely creepy. Everyone knows the shlocky remake with Vincent Van Gogh, but this rare original has been strangely overlooked by historians. British history-making at its best.

1760 **The Industrial Revolution**. Slime 'n' grime and Trooble at t' Mill.

1769 **Napoleon Bonaparte**. This is the one about the Little Man with Big Ideas.

1776 **The United States**. Great blues, great burgers – pity about the Polish jokes.

1837 **The Victorian Age**. The costumes are naff and the sex is kinky. Worth a glance, though, for the wonderfully tacky lighting effects. All that smoke and fog may have brought life expectancy down to the level of a prawn sandwich, but they must have saved art directors a fortune in dry ice.

1859 **The Origin of Species**. Shock horror! The whole schedule turns out to consist of *Planet of the Apes!*

1899 **Sigmund Freud**. Sigmund is a nice Jewish boy in Johann Strauss's Vienna. But when he meets screwed-up Mr Rat Man, strange things begin to crawl out of the woodwork . . .

1905 **The Theory of Relativity**. Things a bit slow down your way? Nip off for a Weekend Break in a space-rocket – and they get slower still. Geddit? No, nor do we. But watch out for the wacky prof with the fright-wig and the spaniel eyes.

1914 **World War I**. Mud 'n' blud, but what it's all about no one knows.

1917 **Communism**. Well, it seemed like a good idea at the time.

1939 **World War II**. Entirely predictable routine spin-off with bigger bangs – plus Vera Lynn. (See Interview feature: 'Adolf Hitler – my dream bathroom', p. 17.)

1969 **Moon landing**. One small step for them – one large vodka for us, please.

1995 **Meltdown**. How predictable can you get? The biggest switch-off since they canned the Epilogue.

Songs without words

The news that English National Opera were proposing to introduce surtitles, even though they always sing in English, has had much the same effect upon a lot of people as the news of Edgardo's betrayal upon her betrothed in *Lucia di Lammermoor*. They went mad. Hands have been wrung, letters have rained down upon editors. An article in the *Independent* described the decision as 'corporate suicide'. Surtitles, said its author, Mark Pappenheim, result in 'an undue emphasis on "what's going on". As if any real opera was ever about anything as banal as narrative action.'

Verdi, he argued, 'never expected every word to be heard – he tried instead to make a few key words (*parole sceniche*, he called them) really come across – words like *madre, amore, morte*.' Every syllable of Mr Pappenheim's argument was clearly distinguishable.

Apparently ENO agree, because the report, like the report of Edgardo's faithlessness, turns out to be false. The surtitles will be merely an experiment at some performances, to replace signing for the hard of hearing.

When it comes to operatic dialogue, though, even sung in English, we're all hard of hearing. I certainly longed for a surtitle or two during ENO's current *Khovanshchina*. This magnificent production of Mussorgsky's great historical epic, which portrays seventeenth-century Russia's belated emergence from mediaeval barbarism into Peter the Great's slightly more up-to-date variant of it, has (for once) been properly and universally acclaimed by the critics. But, as they have also noted, its plot is as tangled as tights in a washing machine.

This is not the fault of the production, or of ENO (who have provided no less than three separate accounts of the plot in the programme, together with an excellent historical background and the genealogy of the Romanovs). It caused me particular difficulties, though. I saw it with a group of friends who in each interval flatteringly turned to me, as someone who knows Russian, and asked me to tell them – well, yes – what was *going on*.

Who were the Streltsy, they demanded. Why were they Archers in some versions, and Musketeers in others? Why did Khovansky appear to be supporting the Tsar in Scene One, and then getting murdered by him in Scene Five? Which side was Golitsyn on? Which side was anyone on? What did the Old Believers believe? Who was this Susanna who suddenly appears out of nowhere in Scene Three and started hurling accusations around? Had she and Figaro fled to Moscow to escape the attentions of Almaviva? Why were there three accounts of the plot in the programme?

My knowledge of Russian didn't help me very much, since it was being sung in English. For myself, of course, I am far above any banal interest in the narrative content of opera, but my companions seemed to place an undue emphasis on the question, even without surtitles to encourage them, and my reputation and authority declined from interval to interval.

It was not as if I hadn't prepared myself – I'd read the three accounts of the plot in the programme, and studied two different works of reference in advance. All five versions went out of my head as soon as the curtain went up. I listened hard for any helpful *parole sceniche*. But you needed a little more to go on in this case than *madre*,

amore, morte. You were hoping for something more like
'. . . son of Tsar Fyodor III's father Alexei not by Maria
Miloslavskaya but by Natalia Naryshkina . . . Vasili Gri-
gorievich, arrested on false testimony for plotting to
usurp the deputy-chairmanship of the Moscow City
Council Cleansing Department . . . Grigory Vasilievich,
supposed second cousin of the disgraced ex-sub-Metro-
politan of Kiev . . .'

But the bits you actually do catch on these occasions
tend not to be quite as *sceniche* as you require. They're
more usually things like: 'Alas . . . Extraordinary to
relate . . . nevertheless . . . Aha . . .! Oho . . .! Oh . . .!
Ah . . .!' (Because of course there's nothing singers sing
more distinctly than open vowel sounds, unconstrained
by consonants.) Also: 'Who is this . . .? What are you
saying . . .? What is *going on* . . .?' Because probably the
characters can't catch much more than we can of what's
being said. Most of them in *Khovanshchina* are also illit-
erate – they haven't even been able to read the programme.

If only Mussorgsky, who wrote his own libretto, had
realised that opera wasn't about anything as banal as
narrative action he could have saved himself, the singers,
and us a great deal of trouble. The discovery has certainly simplified the titanic struggle I have been having
with my commission from ENO to write the libretto for
Euroshchina, Harrison Birtwistle's vast new historical
opera about the crucial negotiations involved in the
emergence of the European Union in its present form.

In this mighty confrontation of historical forces as I
now conceive it, the singers will make up their own text
as they go along in all the inaudible sections, with as
many open vowels and as few consonants as they like.
All I'm going to provide them with is the audible bits.
The job's as good as done.

Act I. *The Grand' Place in Brussels. A vast crowd of under-secretaries, lobbyists, political columnists, disgruntled pig-farmers, speechwriters, and Autocue drivers is surging colourfully around, singing with great conviction about some policy they are strongly in favour of, possibly connected with set-aside payments for turnips, possibly with standardised inflation pressures for children's balloons. A bloody confrontation ensues with another crowd who are strongly opposed to it.*

Enter LANCELOT HIGGLE *(baritone), a journalist who can usually be relied upon for a few quick pars of historical background, to fill us in on the development of the Union so far.*

HIGGLE   (*espansivo*)
Ah! Long and meandering is the path
That led us hither . . . You recall
The basket of currencies . . . the
    shadowed Mark . . .
(Not Mark Thatcher – another one . . .)
But long, long before . . . joint working-
    parties at ministerial level. . . .
Agenda . . . referenda . . . An end
To centuries of conflict . . . Alsace-
    Lorraine . . .
Franco-Prussian War . . .
Holy Roman Empire . . . Huns . . .
    Gauls . . .
Neolithic peoples . . . Ah! Oh . . .!
500 words; invoice follows.

He drinks himself to death. Enter the COMMISSIONER *of some country whose identity is completely obliterated by a blast on the trombones just as his name is announced. He is deep in conversation with a* SECRET

EMISSARY FROM THE CZECH REPUBLIC. *Unless it's* A COM-
PLETE IMBECILE TO CHECK THE PLUMBING.

COMMISSIONER	(*molto moderato*)
	Annexe B to Directive 5Z9 . . .
	Revised draft . . . Amendment
	To Clause 15g . . .
	Your Government's views . . .?
EMISSARY	Ah!
COMMISSIONER	Are? This is most interesting . . .
	Are what?
EMISSARY	Aha!
COMMISSIONER	Are hard? And fast? I see . . .
	Well – a helpful and constructive
	exchange of views . . .
	So vital . . . maintaining a dialogue . . .
	Each other's point of view . . .
EMISSARY	What?
COMMISSIONER	Remarkably . . . For the time of year . . .

Enter HUGH PAYNE *(tenor), a British MP who was intending to vote for the European budget, but who failed to
hear the division bell because of a sudden tutti. Unless
it's* BILL *someone (bass), who was going to vote against,
but who failed to hear the voice of conscience for much
the same reason.*

COMMISSIONER	. . . Hugh Payne?
PAYNE	Who's paying? Who's paying what . . .?
COMMISSIONER	I mean, you're Bill . . . You're Bill . . .
PAYNE	My bill? What bill? Not my bill at the
	Ritz . . .?
COMMISSIONER	The writs . . .? What's this about writs?
PAYNE	. . . Issuing 'em!
COMMISSIONER	Bless you.

Enter LUCIA DI LAMMERMOOR.

48

LUCIA   I seem to be . . . a little confused . . .
                                  Could somebody tell me . . .
                                  What . . . in a word . . . is going on?

Everyone comes surging hopefully downstage and gazes up into the darkness above the proscenium arch. But, fortunately for the aesthetic purity of Europe, up there nothing is going on at all.

A pleasure shared

Do you spit? No? You don't mind if I do, though...?

Khhghm... Hold on – can you see a spittoon on the table anywhere...? Never mind. Sit down, sit down! I can use my empty soup-bowl. Khhghm – *thpp*!

My God, that's better. No, I've been sitting here all the way through the first course just dying for one. Iron self-control, but I do think it's rather bad manners to spit while one's eating. I mean, at a dinner-party like this. Your mouth full of the hostess's soup, and suddenly... kkhghm – *thpp*!

You *have* finished yourself, haven't you? You haven't! I'm so sorry...! Oh, you don't want the rest.

Very nice of you not to... khhghm – *thpp*!... not to mind. One has to be so careful these days not to offend people's prejudices. I always ask first, of course. People never raise any objection, in my experience. In fact they usually never say anything at all. They generally do what you did – smile rather charmingly and kind of wave their hand about. Quite surprised even to be asked, I think, most of them.

Khhghm... Where's the soup-bowl gone...? No, no – sit down! Don't keep jumping up! I'll use yours! You did say you'd finished...? *Thpp*!

I'm glad you're not one of these hysterical people who try to stop other people enjoying themselves. It's so one-sided. I don't try to stop anyone *not* spitting over me! In fact this is something I feel rather strongly about. People used to spit all the time in the good old days, and no one so much as raised an eyebrow. Spittoons everywhere you went – sawdust on the floor. It was only about fifty years ago, you know, that all this anti-spitting nonsense started. Suddenly everyone went mad. Notices up in the buses – 'No Spitting. Penalty £5.' And before we knew what had happened we'd lost another of our ancient liberties.

So, quite honestly, I . . . Khhghm . . . Oh, they've taken the soup-bowls away . . . No, no, stay right where you are! *Thpp*! . . . Keeps the moth out of the tablecloth . . . Yes, I spit very largely as a matter of principle.

And I hawk. As you can hear. Khhghm . . .! In fact I hawk deeply, also as a matter of principle. *Khhhhhghhhhm* . . .! Because I believe that if you're going to spit you might as well get the full benefit of it, and shift the entire contents of your lungs out into the atmosphere. Why keep all that stuff festering inside you, when you could so easily . . . Khhghm – *thpp*! . . . spread it around a bit . . .?

Didn't spit in your face then, did I? Hold on – I think I did! I'm so sorry. I'll just give it a wipe with the corner of the tablecloth . . . Come back, come back! The tablecloth's perfectly . . . no, sorry, hold on, I'll try another bit . . . There we are. It's very nice of you to go on smiling about it, but I know even the most broad-minded non-spitters sometimes feel a little sensitive about getting a faceful of the stuff.

Anyway, point taken! I'll be very careful henceforth to turn my head aside, look, and . . . Khhghm – thpp! . . . spit in your very lovely hair, or down your very charming dress.

Why don't I sit a little closer? There . . . It's the alluring way you're . . .. khhghm – *thpp*! . . . wriggling around! I beg your pardon . . .? It tickles? What tickles . . .? You mean it ran down inside your dress? It gets everywhere,

51

doesn't it! Anyway, don't worry. Just hang your underwear up in some airy place when you get home tonight, and it'll be dry in no time.

Look, you wouldn't mind, would you, if . . . No, come here! Don't lean away! I'm trying to whisper a few private words in your ear. You wouldn't mind, would you, if I gave you a ring some time? I thought perhaps you might like to come round one evening. I could give you a quiet spot of . . . Khhghm – *thpp*! Or we might go out and do something a little more exciting. I don't know. Maybe – Khhghhkhkhkhm – *thppshmk*!

You keep shaking your head. Did you get some in your ear? Don't worry – it's not as if you were inhaling it . . . What? Oh, you're saying no? I see. I see. You're not somehow offended because you got a tiny bit in your eye . . .? I *thought* so! I thought that smile of yours was beginning to get a little fixed. My God! I did *ask*, if you remember. I did ask if you minded!

So you're one of these anti-spitting fanatics, are you? I'm not allowed to spit – is that what you're telling me? – but it's perfectly all right for you to go round leaning away from people, and grinning that ghastly glassy grin at them.

God, the *intolerance* of you lot! It makes me want to . . . Well, I'll tell you what it makes me want to do. It makes me want to *khhhhhhghhhhhm* – Oh, and here's the next course. I'll put that one back for later.

The cogitations of the Earl of Each

Sometimes, as I sit beside the little electric fire in the morning-room, with *The Times* sports pages open beside me, and Henry muttering quietly to himself in his sleep at my feet, I fall into what I call my *cogitational* mood. At these moments it begins to seem to me a matter of some wonder that things are as they are and not otherwise.

Everything! Just thus and so! When it could have been not thus and so at all! Indeed, it could have been not thus and so in various different ways. In a thousand different ways, when you think about it – while there is only the one single way in which things could have been thus and so in the way that they are.

The horse has come in at a thousand to one!

*

And every time I begin to think like this it seems to me that the most surprising thing of all is that I am the Earl of Each.

I. Not my brother Charles or my cousin Shandon. Not some complete stranger. Not some Chinese fellow – and there are a great many more Chinese fellows in the world than there are cousins of mine. Not to mention brothers, of whom there are only three.

None of these people is the Earl of Each. I am. And of me there are even fewer than there are of brothers, let alone cousins or Chinese. Of me there is only one.

Good God.

And here's another thing which is almost as remarkable.

Not only am I the Earl of Each, but the Earl of Each is what I am.

I am not, for example, Sir Alfred Upward. Nor the Marquess of Hight. I am not my brother Charles, nor my cousin Shandon, nor the estimable Wun Hung Lo, nor yet the redoutable Hoo Flung Dung. I am the Earl of Each. No less. No more.

And this astonishing fact is something that everyone takes absolutely for granted. Never has my cousin Shandon said to me: 'Good heavens, Pot, you are the Earl of Each!'

Most of the time I take it pretty much for granted myself.

The Earl of Each. Goodness. I am. My word. The twelfth earl, moreover. Not the eleventh or the thirteenth. The twelfth. Just so. Just exactly so.

*

How has this surprising state of affairs come about?

It is because my father, in his day, could say the same.

So now we must think what it was like for him. And if it is cause for wonder that *I* am the Earl of Each, then it was no less cause for wonder that *he* was the Earl of Each before me. So look here, this isn't a matter of a single horse coming in at a thousand to one! This is the Spring Double!

Another question comes knocking at my brain immediately: how was it that my father was the Earl of Each? It was because *his* father was the Earl of Each before him! And back we go in time to the beginning of the line, wonder before wonder, each as astonishing as the one before it. A tower of improbability twelve floors high!

What we are discussing is not simply the Spring Double. It is nothing less than a twelve-horse accumulator!

*

I sometimes even wonder if we can stop at the first earl. Would Sir George Shy, as he then was, have been created earl if he had not been Sir George? Evidently not, since it was indeed Sir George and no one else who was so created!

Now, would Sir George have been Sir George if his father had not been the father he happened to be? No, plainly, he would have been someone else altogether!

Back we plunge through the centuries to Adam, or the apes!

Yes, and which do I find it easier to believe? That my being the Earl of Each is the final product of God's purpose for the world, or that it results from the blind interaction of chance and natural selection?

I have to confess that I find both hypotheses a little difficult to accept.

*

Another thing: my earldom is a perfect *fit*. At least as good a fit as my shirts and shoes, and a rather better one than my suits, because that fool Stubbs insists on cutting the bellyband of all my trousers too wide – to allow, as he says, for natural development, while never making accommodation for any *other* natural development – for example, the settling of the head forwards and away from the collar that occurs as the years go by, so that I look like a tortoise in its shell.

I wasn't absolutely sure about the earldom when I first came into it, I have to confess, any more than I was with the Oxford brogues that Tapsell made me at about the same time. It took a little while for those shoes to settle to my feet, I recall, but settle they did, just as Tapsell said they would, closer and closer, and it's the same with the earldom. The Earl of Each has become more exactly who I am with every passing day. The bellyband of my earldom, unlike the bellyband of my suits, neither sags nor presses, the collar stays close to my shirt.

And yet it fitted my father before me, who was of a very different temperament from me. In the first place he was not, so far as I know, given to these cogitational moods of mine. It made no difference, though. Earl of Each he was, no less than me.

It fitted his father before him, and his father's father before that.

An amazing garment!

Unless – a new and most striking thought – unless it is not the earldom that ever more closely fits me, but I who ever more closely fit the earldom!

I believe the truth is this – that we have both changed. Just as Henry and I have both changed and accommodated ourselves to each other's ways. He has learnt not to disturb me in my pensive moods; he opens one eye and glances up from the toecap of my shoe, and knows at once that the toecap of my shoe is where he must remain while the mood is upon me, that he must not think of aspiring to rest his head upon my knee. While I, for my part, have learnt not to disturb *his* thoughtful moments by any sudden withdrawal of my foot from beneath his head.

But now a different question arises: am I master or am I dog? I mean, figuratively speaking, in the relationship between me and the earldom. Am I the one sitting by the electric fire with the earldom drowsing on my brogues, or am I down upon the floor, with my chin supported by the tolerance and patience of the earldom above me?

Henry's looking up at me now. I believe he's a little anxious on my behalf. Yes! Deep waters we're getting into here, Henry!

Or is he thinking: 'What surprises *me* is that I am Henry and he is the twelfth earl'?

Back to sleep, Henry!

*

Today, at the fresh fish counter in Tesco's, I met Wiggy Hight, buying prawns for those cats of his. 'Hello, Pot,' he said. It occurred to me that had the world been a slightly different place I should have been the one who was saying 'Hello, Pot'. Then I should have been returning to that dreadful old ruin of his at Godforth and sitting in front of the fire thinking: 'Goodness me, I'm the Marquess of Hight!'

I was very struck by this, but kept my counsel. 'Hello, Wiggy,' I said. I was struck, though, very struck.

*

Well, let us imagine that things *were* arranged differently!

I am imagining as an experiment that I am not an earl at all. Not even a marquess. I am ... Who am I? Yes, I am Fred Upward! Now, here's a laugh.

Let's see ... I'm all skin and bone. I look down at my shoes. Are they Oxford brogues? Not at all, they're mildewed carpet slippers. All right so far. The telephone rings. 'Upward here,' I say. Good. I'm doing rather well so far! Master of disguise!

Hold on, though. Not so fast. Is this still me or isn't it? Is this the Earl of Each telling the world he's Sir Alfred Upward? No, no, everything's changed – I'm old

Fred himself in this arrangement of things! This is Sir Alfred Upward saying he's Sir Alfred Upward.

In which case ... In which case where do we stand? Where do *I* stand? Nowhere, evidently! I seem to have dropped out of the picture completely. In any case Fred's always answering the phone as things are and saying 'Upward here'. So nothing's changed at all!

Who's on the other end of the phone, anyway? Me, in all probability!

By which, of course, I mean the Earl of Each.

*

I realise that these reflections will be of little interest to others. I raised the matter once with Nippy. We were sitting quietly on the terrace after dinner one warm summer evening, enjoying the scent of the tobacco plants. I felt an unusual sense of quiet understanding between us. 'My love,' I said, 'has it ever occurred to you that if things were not as they are, and I were not who I am, then you in your turn would not be who you are?' She didn't reply. I had the impression that she was thinking about it, though. She is not greatly given to abstract thought, so I tried to put the matter in more concrete terms. 'Suppose, for the sake of argument,' I said, 'that I were Alfred Upward. Then you, my love, would be Lady Upward instead of Lady Each.' Another silence ensued. But all she said at the end of it was: 'I think Henry needs worming.'

I tried to discuss it once with Shandon. We were in the butts at Wiggy's, and the birds were remarkably sparse. I put it very simply, in terms of which gun was in whose hands. 'Well, Pot,' said Shandon, 'you always were the brains of the family. So I don't think you can be *this* gun, because I'm pretty sure there's not much in the way of brains lurking about over here.'

Curious that it doesn't strike other people, too. After all, the consequences of my being the Earl of Each are almost as considerable for Nippy and Shandon as they are for me. They reach out to our children, and our children's children. They go on down the generations, for ever and ever.

*

I am the *Earl of Each*. And then again, *I* am the Earl of Each. But every now and then, when my thoughts run very deep, I find yet another cause for wonder – that I *am* the Earl of Each.

Is this less surprising than the first two things, or even more so? But this deep I cannot think for long without fear of never coming to the surface again.

*

Another plunge into deep waters!

If it is against long odds that I am the Earl of Each, how much longer are the odds against the Earl of Each being me.

I'm not making a muddle here, am I? I'm not simply recogitating the same cogitation that I've cogitated before?

I don't believe so. After all, there would have been an Earl of Each sitting here in front of the fire in the morning-room now whenever my dear mother and father had seen fit to begin their eldest son. He might have been a month older than me, or a month younger. He might been a completely different age altogether, and an inch shorter, with darker hair and a less ruddy complexion. He would still have been the Earl of Each, if he was my father's son.

But he wouldn't have been me.

For the Earl of Each to be *me*, the actual fellow who

59

as it happens is indeed sitting here now and cogitating these particular cogitations, then there was only one night in all the years that my parents were married that would serve. I believe this lengthens the odds by another five or six thousand times.

Good God, once again.

Supposing my father had gone up to the House that day, as he sometimes did when some measure relating to land drainage or bloodstock was under discussion, and had stayed overnight at his club! The fellow sitting in this chair now, the present Earl of Each, would have been another fellow altogether!

I feel decidedly peculiar at the thought.

Yes, Henry, well may you look at me like that! Well may you speculate!

Enough!

Come on, dog – a turn around the lake before lunch.

Let us hold on to one absolute and unfailing certainty, Henry, amidst all the dark seas of speculation and conjecture. Let us plant our colours in this one thought and never strike them: that I, old dog of mine, that I, I, am the Earl of Each.

The manual writer's manual

Congratulations! You are a highly-qualified expert in various scientific fields, and you have just been engaged by some leading electronics corporation or software manufacturer to write the instruction manual and Help files for their product. This simple step-by-step guide will assist you to get the most out of your career.

This is an interactive programme. Convenient gaps have been left between the various sentences so that you can stop and go back at any point if you have not understood.

Lesson 1. The purpose of this lesson is to calm your fears about the difficulties of the subject, and to foster a sense of optimism about the work in hand. So:

a. Unscrew the top of your fountain pen. (If you are intending to write your manual on a word-processor, open the instruction manual supplied.)

b. Test that there is ink in the pen. (For word-processor users: read the opening sections of the manual, which you will find are encouragingly simple to understand.)

c. Feel rather pleased with yourself. Wonder why anyone ever thought there was much to writing instruction manuals for leading electronics corporations and software manufacturers.

Lesson 2. The purpose of this lesson is to help you preserve some sense of mystery in your manual. (Hint: for many of your readers technology is taking the place of traditional religious belief. In the past they might have been reading the Scriptures; now they are dependent upon your work to learn an attitude of respect towards the deeper unknowability of the universe, and of deference towards authority – particularly yours!) So:

a. Unscrew the top of your fountain-pen again, if you replaced it at the end of Lesson 1, and

b. Suddenly introduce some quasi-hieratic protocol. If this should cause problems, maximise the heuristic opacity of the procedure by ellipsis or recursiveness in the hermeneutics. The sudden contrast with the somewhat pleonastic exegesis adumbrated in the prolegomena . . .

(Yes, I haven't forgotten it's an interactive programme, and I can see you've got your hand up. Just wait till we get to the end of the sentence.)

> . . . will induce in the neophyte a characteristic disorientation and frustration similar to the feelings notoriously engendered in a child by the unpredictable alternation of maternal love and punishment.

All right. You're confused. Don't worry! You can go back to the beginning at any point. So . . .

Congratulations! You are a highly-qualified expert in various scientific fields, and you have . . .

What . . .? Oh, you understood that bit . . . You mean further on? All right . . .

Unscrew the top of your fountain-pen . . .

No? You don't mean *quasi-hieratic protocol* . . .? Oh, I see . . . No – not the slightest objection to explaining. A *quasi-hieratic protocol* is an expression introduced into the discourse by the initiate without vouchsafed profane signification, with the intention of preserving sacerdotal prerogative. All right . . .?

What do I mean by *an expression introduced into the discourse etc* . . .? I mean an expression such as *quasi-hieratic protocol*.

No, I'm sorry – I'm not going to explain it again. I've already given you a simple ostensive self-referential formulation which I should have thought was comprehensible to a child of $\sqrt[3]{8}$ . . . Yes, certainly – it's an interactive manual. But interactivity doesn't mean constant interruption! It doesn't mean asking about things that I understand perfectly well.

Now, where was I? Yes – and you might like to note this – I was telling you to *maximise the heuristic opacity of the procedure by ellipsis or recursiveness in the hermeneutics* . . . And before you open your mouth again, please don't ask me what heuristics and hermeneutics are! Look them up for yourself! You're a big grown-up scientist!

No, no – I'm not going to tell you where to look them up . . .! All right, then, don't whine – under Epistemology. For heaven's sake! Come *on* . . .!

Where's Epistemology? How should I know? In the back of the book somewhere. In the index. You want me to write the index for you, as well as everything else? Somebody else is doing that! Some specialist index-writer . . .! No, I *don't* look to see what he's put in his index . . . No, he *doesn't* read the text before he writes the index. He's an index-writer, not a manual-reader . . . What does he put in his index? The same as any other writer puts into what he writes! Whatever comes into his head! Which in his case I should think is more probably words like 'fountain-pen' and 'congratulations', because if I know anything about index-writers he's as baffled as you are.

Keep calm, keep calm! There's no need to raise your voice! They did explain to you in the shop, did they, that you need at least a degree in semantics to run this programme . . .? They didn't? Oh, I see. Never mind, press on, do the best we can with the material we've got. So, just check that you *have* taken the top off your fountain-pen . . . Right, good, well done, don't shout. Now, simply bring the nib of the fountain-pen into contact with the paper – right? – and *introduce the crypto-hieratic whatever it was*!

What? Speak up . . . I know, I know – I said *quasi-hieratic* before. I've changed my mind . . . What's the difference? That's my business. It's *my* mind I've changed, not yours. *I* know what I'm talking about . . .

Look, don't scream at me! This is the way manuals are written! I can't change the system! Pull yourself together! You're behaving in a most extraordinary manner. Lying down and drumming your heels on the floor like that! This may be an interactive programme, but interactive doesn't mean screaming abuse, and it doesn't mean hurling the manual across the room. It affords me a certain pleasure to watch you, it's true – but interactive goes both ways, you know. No pudding for you this evening unless you stop this tantrum. My word, even if I did know what pseudo-hieratic whichwhats are I shouldn't tell you now, not after the way you've behaved.

I mean proto-hieratic . . . Or rather hiero-proleptic . . . No . . . What am I talking about? You're getting *me* confused now!

Don't snivel. You'll see the point of all the suffering you've endured in the course of your education when you go out into the world at the end of it and make your own pupils' lives a misery in their turn.

No one could be kinder

You hear a lot about the growing harshness of life. You don't hear so much about the good side of things, though – the huge increase there has been in politeness and kindness.

In the old days, if you rang up Associated Swill Industries, what did they say? They said 'Associated Swill Industries.' Just like that. 'Associated Swill Industries.' Take it or leave it. Or more probably just 'Ndustries'. Because people on switchboards frequently didn't bother to turn on their microphones until they'd almost finished explaining who they were, so you were always talking to firms call 'Umpany', or 'Orporated', or 'Imited'.

It's completely different nowadays. 'Thank you for calling Associated Swill Industries!' they cry, with absolute delight. You're taken aback. You hadn't realised you were doing *them* a favour. You suddenly feel a warm glow, a slight lump in your throat. So, someone in this world does appreciate the efforts you make after all! Your ears are red. 'That's all right,' you feel like mumbling. 'Don't mention it. My pleasure. Least I could do. Any time.'

But before you can say anything – on they go again. 'In what way may I help you?' they say – and you know, from the sheer eager eloquence of the words, that they really mean it. This is astonishing – you scarcely know these people! You find yourself saying: 'Well, I wouldn't mention it if I could think of any other way of doing it – but if you could possibly – I know this is a lot to ask

– but I should be eternally grateful if you could somehow, well . . . *put this call through for me.*'

You were going to say 'To Customer Accounts' – you have a query about your bill. But now the words die on your lips. If someone takes the trouble to talk to you as lengthily as Associated Swill Industries now have, if they have told you how grateful they are to you, and begged you to tell them of any way in which they could possibly make your life better, then you can't just ask for Customer Accounts and start niggling about your bill. They offer you the moon – and you ask for Customer Accounts! It's an inadequate response. It's worse than that – it's a deliberate rebuff, a cold refusal of intimacy.

You feel you should explain about your personal problems. Ask them for advice about where to go on holiday, and how to get on with your parents-in-law – perhaps even request a small unsecured personal loan. Or would this be going too far? You've only known them for such a short while, after all. Though it seems much longer. In fact you suddenly feel as if you had been sitting there talking to Associated Swill Industries for half your life. So you ask if they could possibly put you through not to anywhere as mundane as Customer Accounts, but to the Chairman himself.

Then you can threaten him with legal action for the amount of your time and your capacity for emotional response that his firm has wasted.

I'm also rather overcome when people I've never met before tell me, usually over a public address system, often on aircraft, that I'm *kindly requested* to do this, or not do that. In the bad old days they used to say, 'Will you kindly do this? Will you kindly not do that?' In other words they expected all the kindness to be provided by us in doing as they asked. Why should *we* have to start laying out stocks of kindness, when we're not getting paid for it? Particularly when we'd no idea in what spirit the request was being made. Were they requesting us kindly? Or were they doing it unkindly? Quite unfeelingly, perhaps – cruelly, even? And then they expect us to be kind to *them*!

Now we know that a warm heart and a generous nature are concealed behind that loudspeaker. I just wonder, though, if it's fair that they should have to tell us this themselves. Suppose there was no one to introduce a distinguished visiting lecturer, and he had to start off by telling us himself how witty and erudite he was, and how he was going to enlighten and entertain us!

Couldn't some of the switchboard operators who have spent so much time helping callers that their employers have gone into receivership – couldn't they travel aboard planes and introduce the speakers? They wouldn't be hampered by any lingering modesty. 'Mr Clake, your Director of Passenger Services, is known wherever aircraft fly not only for the kindness with which he makes his requests, but also for the refined accent that he does it in. Critics have praised the sheer courage and determination of his requesting, its exuberance, its technical virtuosity – and at the same time its engaging modesty. So, here, to ask you to leave the aircraft by the forward exit – the great requester himself! Ladies and gentlemen, will you please welcome – Mr Clake!'

Politeness hangs in the air these days even when there's no one there to utter it. It's not just switchboard operators who thank you for calling them – so do answering machines. Slot machines thank you for putting money into them. Tills send you courteous little bread-and-butter letters, as if you'd had them to stay for the weekend.

Towns and villages have been welcoming arriving motorists for many years – even at night, even in the rain, when there's no one around, and all the petrol stations and cafés are shut. But now so do railway stations. Welcome to Wolverhampton (High Level)! they cry silently. Welcome to West Wittering! The grimy paintwork is attempting to smile, the empty fire-buckets seem to be offering flowers. As they get the technology of politeness better even small suburban stations, deserted in the freezing dusk, will bank up the fire in the waiting-room for us. Invite us to stay to dinner with the vending machine. They are but humble establishments, notices will explain, but we should be welcome to share their modest fare, if we don't mind a simple bag of crisps, perhaps washed down with a cup of the local instant tea, or instant cocoa if we'd be kind enough to press the button on the right. They would account it an honour if we would spend the night on one of their broken benches, alongside any other derelicts who haven't yet been moved on by the police.

They do mean it all, do they? They're not just saying these things?

I'd be happier if they could offer us some reassurance about the spirit they were saying them in. 'You are kindly welcomed,' the notices on the stations might say. 'You are eloquently thanked,' the till receipts might cry. 'And we say this with absolute sincerity and deep conviction! If we had eyes there would be real tears in them! If we had hearts they would be overflowing most painfully! How can mere stove-enamelled signs, mere scraps of printed paper, adequately bear witness to the turbulence of the emotions surging through our keyboards, raging through our public conveniences? You are kindly requested to look in the till and see for yourself how full its heart is! You are benevolently begged to listen to the wind howling through the broken windows of the ticket-office, and hear for yourself its genuine sense of pain!'

And, finally convinced, we should fold the receipts carefully away next to our hearts, and press our lips against Network SouthEast's cold and rainswept logo.

He said, she said

'What was that?' he said suddenly.

She looked up sharply, frightened by the alarm in his voice.

'I thought I saw . . .' he began, then stopped. 'There they are again!' he said softly. 'Yes, and now there's two more of them!'

He seemed to be trying to brush something away from around his face, like a man bothered by flies. There were no flies, however. She looked around her uneasily.

'I can't see anything . . .' she began, but then stopped in her turn, because no sooner had she uttered the words than she could. She could see them quite clearly. They were very small, but for an instant their heads and their characteristic curving tails were absolutely distinct.

'You, too?' he said.

She nodded.

'Yes,' she replied grimly, brushing them away from her hair. 'Inverted commas. Quotation marks.'

'Right,' he agreed. 'And not just the odd couple, here and there. They're all around us. Swarms and swarms of them.'

'Well,' she said. 'We both know perfectly well what it means. The fact is, we're in the middle of a passage of dialogue.'

'Oh God,' he agonised softly.

'I know,' she sympathised. She put her hand on his arm for a moment and smiled at him. He managed a smile in return.

There seemed to be nothing more to say.

*

Many long paragraphs of narrative and description followed during which not a word was uttered. Then:

'They're back,' he said.

'So I see,' she replied, trudging on without looking up. 'But I think the thing is to pay no attention – just to get on with other things at the same time and keep ourselves distracted.'

She took out a few useful gerunds that she always kept with her, and passed a handful to him.

'You mean, saying what one has to say,' he said, running his hand reflectively through his thinning hair, 'and at the same time doing something like running one's hand reflectively through one's thinning hair?'

'Yes, or fixing the person you're talking to with a gaze that goes on and on,' she suggested, fixing him with a gaze that went on and on.

'I see,' he said, not seeing at all.

'Or even just thinking something to yourself, or feeling some sort of feeling,' she went on, thinking to herself that he wouldn't even know that she *was* thinking to herself, and feeling rather pleased about it. 'Though it doesn't even have to be a gerund,' she went on, throwing in another gerund all the same.

'How do you mean?' he asked, wrinkling his forehead in a puzzled frown.

'You can just put in a full stop and then do something else,' she replied. She put in a full stop, just like that, with a wonderful insouciance. 'It doesn't even have to have anything to do with what you're saying.' She began to manufacture a double bass out of a pile of firebricks and a ball of pale blue wool. 'Anything, just so long as it holds off the inverted commas for a bit.'

He thought about this in silence. He hated trying to do two different things at once.

'What I've noticed,' he said at last, 'is that even if one doesn't do other things while one's speaking, other things often seem to do themselves.'

As he spoke, an aircraft appeared in the sky, heavily laden with symbolic reference, and crashed portentously behind the pigsties.

*

'*He said*,' he said, a few pages later.

'What?' she said.

'*She said*! There we go again! Didn't you hear it?'

'Oh, that. Yes. You always get that.'

'So who's saying it?' he demanded. 'Who's saying all this *she said* and *he demanded*?'

'Not me,' she shrugged.

'*She shrugged*! Oh, honestly! Before we know where we are we'll be getting *he gritted*.'

There was a slight pause. Then – *he expostulated*.

They stopped talking and listened for some moments, waiting to hear what variations they would be reduced to next. But nothing happened. There was silence.

'I can stand the inverted commas . . .' he began, and stopped. 'There it goes again – *he began*! Every time I open my mouth! It's getting on my nerves.'

'It's as if someone was listening in to everything we said,' she complained.

'It's so unnecessary, that's what maddens me.'

'Everyone knows we're saying things. They don't have to keep being told.'

'Just a moment, though . . .'

'What?'

'I think it's stopped!'

'Has it . . .? Yes, so it has!'

'They must have realised we could hear them.'

'Well, thank heavens for that!'

'Yes . . . Only . . .'

'Only what?'

'Well, this is rather silly, but I've forgotten which of us is which.'

'Which of us is which? That's easy. You just count back to the last *he said* or *she said*.'

'Oh, I see. Hold on, then . . . You, me, you, me . . . Or, just a moment, was it Me, you . . .? No, no – I know – You, me, you, me, you, me, you, me . . . Good God – I'm *she*!'

'Don't be silly. Can't you tell from the kind of thing you're saying? That's the way *he* speaks!'

'Is it? Hold on . . . You, me, you, me, you, me, you, me, you . . . Yes! You're she and I'm you! No . . .'

They looked up at the sky, hoping to hear even the faintest *he said* or *she said* echoing through the universe. But the sky was very clear and very empty.

*

For several pages they vanished altogether. Other people took their place, and said this and said that in their turn, and explained and gasped and riposted, and got murdered in various strikingly horrible ways.

'What I really object to,' he said, as soon as they were back, but she stopped him.

'You see?' she said. 'I *knew* it was going to turn out to be you and not me when we got our bearings again. Sorry. Go on.'

'What I object to,' he pursued, 'is being pushed back into the past all the time. When I say something – when I say what I'm saying now, for instance – I feel as if I'm saying it, well, *now*, in the present. But as soon as I've

74

finished – wham! – *he said* – and I realise it was way back in the past. I feel I'm being robbed of my life.'

'I know what you mean,' she said hesitantly. 'But I think one just has to have faith. One has to believe that one day we'll . . . catch up.'

'Catch up?' he queried.

'Get right through the book, to the very last page.' Her eyes were shining. Her eyes were shining because it was an interestingly different way of indicating that she was the one who had been doing the speaking.

'And then at last it will be all *he says* and *she grinds out*?' His ears reddened, for much the same reason as her eyes had been shining.

She shook her head, meaning no, but meaning also that she was the next one to speak.

'No,' she said, just to make it doubly clear. 'But if we can get to the last page we might just get a glimpse of the back of the jacket. Because that's where he lives, this person who keeps saying *he said* and *she said*.'

He looked at her. 'You mean, we might talk to him? Might even shout *he said* every time he opens his mouth?'

She smiled. 'I don't think we'll ever get ahead of him. He's too clever for that. But we might, just for a moment, catch a glimpse of his photograph. We might find out where he went to school, and whether he's married or not.'

And so on they went. Though neither of them knew it yet, they had another 359 pages to go, including 2,769 more *he* and *she said*s, and no less than 4,833 pairs of inverted commas.

So, by the time they got there, the photograph on the back of the jacket would be as out of date as everything else.

Your inattention, please

Now will you please ensure that your seat-belt is securely fastened, ready for take-off.

Your table should be folded away, with the seat-back upright and the arm-rest down. Your mind should be in the closed position to be adopted when routine safety announcements of this sort are made. Faces should be completely obscured by newspapers, or eyes securely shut. If you are still conscious, you may find the level, hypnotic tone of voice in which this announcement is being made helpful in securing complete inattention.

In the pocket in front of you you will find a card showing aircraft safety procedures. In the interest of your own peace of mind, please studiously ignore this. Any attempt to look at it may result in your appearing nervous or inexperienced to your fellow-passengers. We are mentioning it purely as a test to make sure that no one is listening.

The cabin attendants will now demonstrate the use of the aircraft's emergency oxygen masks and lifejackets. They are not trained in mime or the use of theatrical properties, and they find this performance profoundly embarrassing. It is important to them to know that no one is watching. Those of you who are unable to read, or who are afflicted by insomnia, may look out of the window.

If for any reason the cabin air-supply should fail, oxygen will be provided. Masks like this will appear automatically. We say 'like this', but what in fact these masks are like you have of course no idea. In the unlikely event of anyone looking up, and seeing the entire cabin staff transformed into grinning effigies of Prince Charles, please remain seated. Place the newspaper back in front of your face and try to breathe normally.

The action of pulling the mask to the face automatically opens the way to less inhibited behaviour. Please do not smoke when the masks are in use, as the lighted end of the cigarette may be forced up your nostril.

There are emergency exits on both sides of the aircraft. They are not being pointed out to you now, because they are clearly marked. It is true that the cabin attendants are swinging their arms forwards and sideways, but this is part of a simple programme of physical exercise intended to relieve stress caused by the frustration inherent in the nature of the work.

Additional lighting is provided on the arm of your seat and at floor level for the convenience of passengers who have sunk even deeper behind their newspapers at this time.

In the unlikely event of a landing on water, you will find that you have no idea where your life-jacket is stowed. If this should happen, remove outer clothing and prepare for immersion. Place your jacket carefully under the seat in front of you, check that your shirt is free from the waistband of the trousers or skirt, then pull it upwards over the head in one steady movement, like this.

It is particularly important that no one watches any part of what follows.

Release the catch at the waistband, pull down the fastener provided, and let the lower garments fall to the floor. Please ensure that they do not obstruct the emergency exits.

There is a whistle attached to your lifejacket for

77

attracting attention, which attendants are holding close to their lips, but being very careful not actually to blow in case attention should indeed be attracted. In a real emergency this would of course be still under your seat with the lifejacket, and you may wish to try alternative methods of persuading people to look at you.

Your cabin attendants are now demonstrating the procedure for these. Ladies should undo the fastenings at the front of the upper undergarment as shown, and pass it backwards over the shoulders, like this.

Now, peel any hosiery downwards, like this, followed by the lower undergarment, taking care to keep the pelvis rotating at the same time, as shown. Once off, the undergarments may if desired be passed around various parts of the body, like this, then tossed lightly into the faces of potential rescuers, who may be engrossed in the *Financial Times* at least as deeply as passengers are now.

If you are still wearing the masks at this time, you may wish to loosen your inhibitions even further, as attendants are now demonstrating.

If necessary, the pressure can be increased by applying the mouth to this mouthpiece, but gentlemen, no pipes or cigars, please. For your own safety and comfort, kindly do not inflame other passengers until you are outside the aircraft.

Thank you for your complete lack of attention. Now please allow cabin staff a few seconds to retrieve their clothes and retire to the galley areas to dress, then open your eyes, fold newspapers away, settle back in your seats and enjoy the flight.

The words and the music

They keep playing *music* on Radio 3, have you noticed?
I find it rather intrusive. You're just settling into a good
long interview with someone, you don't know who,
because you missed the beginning, but he seems to play
the flügelhorn, and you're finding out a great deal about
his childhood in Leicestershire, and his views on Pend-
erecki and the shortcomings of flügelhorn teaching in
England, when they suddenly break off to play some
symphony or concerto.

They keep playing music in concert-halls, too, and I
read somewhere recently that audiences there are also
getting pretty sick of it. What people want, it's been
discovered, is not just musicians playing at them relent-
lessly, it's someone to introduce it all, some familiar personality who can talk them through it.

No one, so far as I know, has yet suggested it in the
opera-house. But it would be the most natural thing in
the world. There tend to be a lot of low moments in operas
after a famous aria ends, when everyone takes a bit of a
break. The composer's thinking up some more tunes for
the next famous aria; the baritone's gone off to have a
cup of tea; a mezzo has come on, and is making small
talk to the soprano about offstage political developments
and the unreliability of the men in their lives; the orches-
tra's vamping till ready, or even off the stand altogether
while the harpsichordist fills in until the next set.

Wouldn't it be much better if they cut all this, and
Michael Aspel or someone, possibly in a costume suitable

to the piece, came on and asked the soprano how things were going in her career? Not in her career as betrayed queen or consumptive courtesan, of which we know only depressingly too much already, but in her career as a soprano, where things will certainly turn out to be going much better.

'Lorraine,' he'd say, 'you've just had a rapturous reception for your wonderful *Non sporgersi*. This was obviously something you've been working towards in your career for some time.'

'Yes, Michael, I've been looking forwards to it ever since the overture. I really felt I was ready for it. Any earlier in Act One and the chorus would still have been singing *Vietato l'ingresso*. Any later and I should have run up against Rodolfo doing his wonderful *Quanto costa*. And everyone has been so tremendously supportive.'

'I couldn't help noticing Sir Edward down there on the rostrum, waving his arms about and really urging you to go for it.'

'Yes, the conductor has always been a great influence on me – particularly in deciding the right moment to attempt something new.'

'I believe your immediate plans include one more aria in Act One?'

'If I can fit it in, Michael. I do have a rather heavy schedule of interview work.'

'Yes, tell me something about that. Is the technique involved very different from singing?'

'Oh, it uses completely different physical apparatus. It puts a tremendous strain on the zygomaticus major and the orbicularis oris.'

'Which of course are the muscles you need for smiling.'

'And which tend as you know to remain under-developed and flabby in the opera repertoire. The strain

80

on them can cause tension in the digastric and stylohyoid – which can in turn affect the chuckle.'

'You are of course known for the amazing sprizzatura of your chuckle. I remember your wonderfully rich, sustained chuckling in Act Three of *La Pastasciutta* in San Francisco, in that famous interview you did with KCFR. But you've had some trouble with your chuckle recently, haven't you?'

'I think it was just the strain of trying to keep up my singing as well as the interviewing. Sometimes the chuckle just wouldn't come.'

'There was one occasion at the Met, I believe . . .?'

'Yes, when I broke down in the middle of an interview, and just started to sing uncontrollably. It was very embarrassing. But I went to a wonderful woman in New York who helped me to see that question and answer are really yin and yang – part of the natural harmony of the universe. I think now I'm interviewing better than ever.'

'You don't intend to give up singing altogether?'

'I hope not. But I can't help feeling that there's so much conflict in opera, so much aggression. Everyone gets tremendously emotional. It's not surprising they keep murdering each other. All they can think about is treachery and despair and death. Whereas now, for instance, we're both able to keep perfectly calm. We can just stand here and have a nice friendly talk about really interesting things, such as my career, and we've both got a chance to show the nice side of our natures. A lot of the characters in opera are frankly not very nice.'

They're having such a nice friendly talk, in fact, that they forget about the audience completely. She pours him some Ribena from one of the golden jugs brought on for the great drinking song earlier in the act. They wander among the cardboard trees in the moonlight, and she asks him what he thinks she ought to do about Rodolfo.

81

Should she wait until Act Three, then simply die of consumption and a broken heart? Or should she make a preemptive strike in Act Two, and have him murdered by hired assassins?

He says that if she and Rodolfo could just stop singing for a moment, and talk to each other quietly, the way he and she are doing now, they might be able to get their problems sorted out.

'You're right,' she murmurs. 'It's the singing – it's the music. It's got to go. Insightful relationships and coloratura just don't mix. I feel I've become a lot more mature about my work in the last few minutes.'

He is fascinated by all this, but he can't help noticing that they are being watched. There is a face just visible out there in the darkness somewhere, with an impatient expression on it. He can see a raised arm, holding some sort of weapon.

'The conductor?' she says. 'Let him wait. I'm tired of being told what to do by conductors. I'm tired of having all my thoughts and feelings laid down for me on staves, measured out by bar-lines. I've got past that stage of my career now.'

Well, they talk for a long time. They have come to share a vision. They want everyone in the world to be interviewed. Not just musicians, but industrialists, generals, postmen, train-drivers. Because if everyone would simply stop *doing* things all the time, if they could just sit down on the scenery and *talk* about it instead, then obviously there would be fewer wars, there'd be less pollution. Letters wouldn't get mis-delivered, trains wouldn't run into each other.

'And the most wonderful thing of all,' they cry out at last in unison, 'is that it would be so much cheaper!'

No one hears this bit, though, because the audience

82

has long since taken their point, and they're all rather noisily interviewing each other.

Eating for others

The beggars you meet in the street these days don't seem to know anything about modern fundraising.

They ask you for money. This is a very naive and counter-productive approach. You know they propose to spend the money entirely on themselves, and no one finds blatant self-interest very appealing. They haven't grasped the essential point of all commercial enterprise, that to make a profit you must first invest. They don't understand that the most effective way to solicit a gift is to offer a gift.

But, you protest, the old man outside Marks and Spencer who keeps asking you for the price of a cup of tea – how can he offer you a gift? He hasn't anything to give! No, but then nor has the Royal National Metropolitan Centre of Cultural Excellence. According to their last published accounts they have about £4 million *less* than the old man outside Marks and Spencer. Has that ever stopped them sending you free glossy brochures, which you put by to read at the weekend, but which then get covered up by the week's newspapers, so that you never even discover there's a quid pro quo in the shape of a banker's order form inside the back cover?

It's not *their* money that they're spending, this is the point. It's *your* money. It's the money you will give them out of the sense of obligation imposed by their giving something to you. Or would have given them, if you hadn't taken their little offering round to the recycling depot first. And *you* have plenty of money. I hope.

Because once I've explained these basic principles to the old man outside Marks and Spencer you're going to need it.

I'm preparing a business pack on the subject, which I shall be giving him instead of money the next time he approaches me. So the next time he approaches *you*, after he has digested my advice, and raised the appropriate venture capital from his merchant banker contacts in the City, he won't ask you for anything.

Instead he will thrust a very large invitation card into your hand, printed in raised italic script, with his family coat of arms at the top embossed in gold. Even before you read it you will feel a simple pride at the thought of being able to prop this thing up casually on your mantlepiece, where its sheer size, and the glitter of its gold embossing, will arouse the envy of every visitor who walks into the room.

When you do read it you will discover that, far from being asked for the price of a cup of tea, you are being offered refreshment yourself. Not only you, but your partner as well. Not on the pavement outside the Kwality Liquor Mart, where this man usually consumes any cups of tea he has been able to raise finance for, but in the banqueting suite of some more central hostelry, such as the Royal Imperial Intercontinental Hotel. Not in the company of him and his fellow tea-drinkers, but in the presence of a Royal Highness.

You talk it over sensibly with your partner, and you decide to invest 25p in a stamp to put on your acceptance, which is probably already 5p more than you would have advanced towards the cup of tea. You take your dinner jacket and evening dress to the cleaners (another £15 or so, but they need cleaning anyway). When you look at the results you make a joint reasoned decision to invest a further £200 in a new evening dress, because you are after all going to be hobnobbing with royalty, and perhaps, if you seem presentable enough, getting invited to some delightful little intimate party they are giving themselves. Then, when the day comes, you spend another £15 on a taxi to get to the Royal Imperial Intercontinental Hotel, because you can't really travel on public transport in your amazing new evening dress, and you don't want to risk driving home still intoxicated by the delightfulness of the royal presence.

You know that at some point, sooner or later, you will be writing a cheque for some not too gracelessly mean amount in return for all this. But what you'll be getting for your money! No question of a cup of tea. You'll be getting champagne and canapes, followed by four courses of food specially rich in health-giving cholesterol, washed down by several different sorts of wine, followed by brandy or liqueurs. You will be entertained by delightful speeches, which various public relations consultants and equerries have given up whole highly-paid days to writing.

The Royal Highness will turn out not to be sitting at your table, sadly, but you will have the pleasure of being among people who seem to be as wealthy as you hope you look yourself. If a gentleman, you will find yourself sitting with a lovely wealthy lady in a new evening dress on either side of you; if a lady, with a distinguished wealthy gentleman in a newly-cleaned dinner jacket. Your head whirls with the possibilities of moneyed romance. Which of your two partners to exchange delicious gallantries with first? You turn gracefully to the one on your left, say, and you talk about . . .

You talk about . . .

About . . . well . . . where he or she lives. You talk about where *you* live. You talk about where you are both going on holiday, the precise numbers of your respective children, their educational arrangements and professional prospects.

Enchanting as this conversation is, you will remember halfway through the *sole avec son coulis de kiwi* that you haven't said anything to your charming and well-heeled companion on the right, so you will turn to him or her. Your tongue loosened now by wine, you will find no more difficulty in finding conversational topics. You will talk about ... where you both live ... where going/gone on holiday ... numbers of children ... children's outstanding charms and achievements ...

By the time you have got on to the *kiwis dans un parfait de chèvre* it will come to you that there is something suspiciously familiar about this person's entire life. Slowly you will realise that you sat next to him or her at some similar occasion last year, and went through precisely the same conversation. In the ensuing silence you will find time to eat three *petits fours* instead of one, and have a brandy, which you never normally do. You may go so far as to take the cigar you are offered, even though you don't smoke, and put another one in your breast pocket or handbag, something you'd noticed other people doing but had never thought you would be bold enough to do yourself.

So you go home with a feeling in your chest which is either heartburn or heart disease, or possibly just the cockles of your heart being warmed by all the good you have done. You pay another £15 for a taxi, or £20 in parking fees, because you couldn't in fact find a taxi when you set out and had to bring the car after all, or £100 to release the car from the car-pound, because you couldn't find a parking-space, plus a £1,000 fine for driving with more than the permitted limit of royal highness in your blood; all of which, together with the loss of your licence and consequently your job, at say £50,000 a year for the next ten years, brings the bill for the evening up to somewhere around half a million pounds.

Not to mention your generous contribution to the organisers of all this, which will at last provide the old man outside Marks and Spencer with his cup of tea, unless all his 20p share of the proceeds has gone in administration.

And you have the pleasant prospect of doing the same thing again the following week, to finance a cup of coffee for the man who usually stands outside Sainsbury's.

Destroy before reading

I wrote a piece a few weeks back in which I expressed some scepticism about a mnemonic that one of my daughters used to have for remembering her personal identity number at work. I subsequently got letters from one or two people who accused me of destroying my daughter's confidence and losing her her job.

Ridiculous, of course. But then I realised that my daughter hadn't said anything about the article herself ... I began to worry. My children have all been amazingly supportive over the years about my professional activities – as scrupulously encouraging as the most devoted parents indulging the most insufferable child. Maybe I *had* been a little heavy-handed, I thought, perhaps even a little insensitive about mentioning the matter at all.

So I rang her to check, and she said she hadn't read the article yet. She'd put it aside to read, she said, but what with work and the children she'd been extremely busy, and they'd got the builders everywhere, and somehow the paper must have got thrown away. To my horror I realised that she had a rather defensive tone in her voice. She had understood my query not as an expression of tender regard for her feelings, but as a reproach for failing in her filial obligations. Not only had I destroyed her confidence and lost her her job – I'd somehow transferred my parental anxieties to her.

This was, needless to say, the last thing I wanted – particularly since I know she scarcely has time to breathe, let alone read newspapers – and since I am in a permanent fever of guilt myself about not having read all the things that people I know have written. I can't! There are too many people writing things, and only me to read them all!

So of course I felt more anxious than ever. To set her mind at rest I made a copy of the article and sent it to her, then forgot the whole matter. I rang her a week later about something else – and before I could speak she said quickly: 'I'm afraid I still haven't read the article yet.'

I said I didn't know what article she was talking about. She said she'd put it carefully away to read as soon as she had the leisure, only what with work . . . Yes, yes, I said. . . . And the children, she said . . . Please, I cried . . . And the house being rebuilt . . .

I said she didn't have to read it. She said she was longing to read it. I forbade her to read it. She said she knew what it was like if you wrote things and people didn't read them. I said I knew what it was like if people wrote things and you felt you had to read them. Etcetera.

By this time I was feeling terrible. I thought of the burden I'd imposed upon all my children. Scribble scribble scribble. Articles, scripts, and advance copies of books piling up accusingly on their plates, like more and more helpings of nightmare strained spinach.

Another week went by. I didn't dare ring my daughter. And when at last I did – on some totally unconnected topic, I most solemnly swear – she confessed that she had now also lost the copy I had sent her. She had filed it carefully away in her kitchen, treasuring it up until she really had time to enjoy it to the full – and the builders had demolished the kitchen!

It seemed to me that this thing was getting entirely out of hand. She'd had to destroy a substantial part of her house to find an excuse! Confidence – job – peace of mind – and now her kitchen – all gone! I ran to the copier, to rush her another copy, if not another kitchen.

Whereupon the copier ceased to function. A small enough punishment for destroying one child's home and livelihood, but it relieved my feelings a little. I called the service engineer. (£45 call-out fee, which relieved them a little further.) He said that according to the meter inside the machine I had made 98,000 copies in the couple of years I had owned it. He implied that I had worked the wretched machine to death. So now I began to feel bad about the copier as well. Not to mention my children. 98,000? Had I forced *that* many copies of articles on them? No wonder they were being driven to such desperate measures!

As soon as he had gone I rushed to the machine again to copy the article, and ease my daughter's burden of guilt, if not mine. And immediately it died again. A curse had fallen upon our entire house! Or what was left of it.

A second engineer came, and operated on the machine for most of the morning. When he emerged from the sickroom he told me that according to the meter I had produced only 1,900 copies in all the time I had owned it. I hadn't used it enough, he said reproachfully. As a result the grease inside had gone cold.

Since then the fax has jammed, the phone has gone on the blink, and the television has packed up. Either I've used them too much, or else I haven't used them enough. I should have given them a proper balance of exercise and rest each day, like dogs, or a string of racehorses. A little light copying, a little light faxing, three times a day, so that they didn't become bored and demoralised and start having breakdowns. Then a blanket over them and a brisk rubdown to stop them getting their grease chilled. And I shouldn't have kept making the fax and the copier read things I'd written.

Then I began to think of all the little machines I have with *batteries* in them. Some of them were lying forgotten in various drawers, their batteries never renewed, so that by now the acid would be corroding their little insides. I thought of all the machines with rechargeable batteries that I had failed to recharge – no, worse! – failed to *dis*charge regularly, so that by now their capacity for holding a charge would be wrecked beyond recall.

And now, of course, I'm starting to worry about my daughter reading *this* article, and feeling that it's somehow her fault that the copier jammed, and the miniature vacuum cleaner for getting dust out of electronic machinery has got corroded, and the laptop won't charge. I'll have to keep it from her somehow.

Blow up the rest of her house, perhaps, just as this morning's paper is delivered. I suppose it's a fairly standard family saga. You start off with a passing remark – you end up with *Götterdämmerung*.

Frox 'n' sox

Theologians now believe that the wide variety of beliefs and practices observable among the different Christian churches must have derived originally from some common source – perhaps from some kind of gospel preached by an itinerant religious leader in the Middle East about two thousand years ago.

What exactly was in this gospel it's very hard to reconstruct. Not all churches, for example, seem to accept central tenets such as a belief in organised violence and the preservation of wealth and privilege. But scholars think they have located the one profound and passionate conviction that they almost all share – a horror of loud ties.

They point to the remarkable unanimity with which the priests of almost every known Christian sect have avoided the wearing of ties of any sort – not only ones with a motif of lightly-clad women or favourite cartoon characters, but even simple stripes signifying membership of the Garrick Club or the Old Haileyburians. Indeed, in their efforts to avoid any temptation to wear unsuitable ties, priests of all denominations have tended to eschew even suits or jackets, at any rate on formal occasions. With striking singleness of mind they have elected to wear frocks.

Scholars are insistent that at no point in the history of the church were frocks ever worn to show off the figure of the wearer, or to titillate in any way whatsoever. The original doctrine, they believe, must have made it clear that the frocks were to be full-length evening gowns, with no hint of décolletage, and no leg showing. Any suggestion of tightness over the hips or around the bosom was to be most sedulously avoided. Black seems to have been thought the safest colour, though brown, grey, and dark blue were evidently regarded as acceptable. Various shades of green have sometimes been tried by the adventurous, but considerable caution must have been recommended with lilac and puce. Red and purple, yes, possibly – but you had to be the kind of person who could carry it off.

The choice of material was another area where discretion had to be exercised. Silk for a really special occasion could be lovely, perhaps with a tasteful embroidered stole thrown around the shoulders. But definitely no sequins, no lamé, no lurex, and nothing diaphanous. Jewellery – yes, certainly, why not, provided it was reasonably discreet. A nice gold chain, perhaps, with something dangly at the breast. A few chunky rings. Not earrings, though, and nothing in the nostril. A hat could be a definite plus – a little pill-box worn at a slightly cheeky angle was always thought to look smart, and you can't really go wrong with a low crown and a broad brim. But no feathers and no veils!

Up to this point the doctrine seems very straightforward and commonsensical. There was another side to it, though, scholars have established, which is more mystical, and which has to be pieced together with great delicacy and sensitivity to metaphysical nuance. This is the question of what was to be worn underneath the frocks.

It was understood that some priests would wish to wear trousers under their skirts and that others would prefer not to. The choice was left entirely to the dress-sense of the individual priest, and his sensitivity to the climate in which he found himself. The crucial question related to socks. It was made plain that socks, if worn, should be thick, woollen, and reasonably short. They should be worn either sagging around the ankles, or supported by strongly-made brass and elastic suspenders somewhere about the mid-calf. They might be obtained from Marks and Spencer, or home-knitted by devoted relatives and parishioners. They were to be, in a word, *male socks*.

Now it was always recognised by Christian doctrine that priests are not the only people in the world who wear frocks. There are others, superficially indistinguishable from priests, who can be told apart only because they wear not male socks under their frocks, but much longer, more exiguous pieces of hosiery, often smooth and diaphanous in texture, and held up not by forthright brass and scarlet elastic around the calf, but by flimsy contraptions of straps and frills emanating from mysterious recesses of underwear which need not concern us here. People with arrangements of this sort under their frocks have therefore often been known as *the weaker socks*.

The reference is purely to the lower tensile strength of the materials, and it must be stressed that the weaker socks have always been recognised as absolutely equal in the sight of God, who has no personal interest at all in people's undergarments. Christians have never been encouraged to go round peering under other people's frocks to see what they are wearing beneath. In fact the various churches have always tended to discourage any very close interest in this whole question. They have never been able to understand why people seem to think of nothing but socks, socks, socks.

Indeed their chief concern has been to keep the two different kinds of socks apart. Those ordained by God to

95

wear thick socks under their frocks, they have felt, should not experiment with silk stockings and high heels. Those born to silk stockings and high heels should not start throwing their frocks off, and going round wearing pinstripe suits and Brigade ties. Trousers, possibly – though preferably short enough to be entirely concealed beneath their frocks. The exact form of these concealed trousers has never been of direct concern to the church, but normal good sense suggests that they should be made not of thick materials like tweed or corduroy, but of silk or cotton, trimmed perhaps with a little lace . . . However, this is straying from the central theological issue.

Which is at all costs to stop the weaker socks wearing the same kind of frocks as the male socks!

This is of vital importance, because otherwise the two different sorts of frocks might get mixed up in church, and it has always been an essential belief that the frocks with the rough woollen socks under them should be kept up one end of the building, and the frocks with the long translucent silk socks under them should be down the other end, with some kind of fence or rail separating them.

This is so that the thick socks can be clearly seen and heard while they explain that anyone having problems about frocks and socks can take heart, because things will be much easier to understand when they are dead. In the next world everyone will be wearing long white frocks and no socks at all, so there will be a very relaxed atmosphere, and a very jolly time will be had by all.

Apart, that is, from those people who have got confused about questions of frocks and socks in this life. If they have, then they *won't* have white frocks when they're dead – they won't have frocks at all – they'll just get flogged and tortured in the nude.

Though if that's what they *like*, if they've been taking

their frocks off and getting themselves flogged and tortured in the nude in *this* life, then very probably they won't get flogged and tortured in the nude when they're dead after all. They'll find themselves *forced* to wear frocks as a punishment, for all eternity.

And horrible tickly socks, with huge holes in them.

We all say the same

Sir – Are we alone in deploring the alarming decline in the number of Letters to the Editor bearing multiple signatures?

No, Sir, we are not alone! At the foot of this letter you will find 270 signatures, standing in proud columns, shoulder to shoulder, united in deploration. (Or 271 if Renforth Ossett BA MBE signs, as he promised Sir Spencer Fough KCVO he would, though we have been unable to confirm this, in spite of many attempts to telephone him.)

We believe that together we are able to deplore far more deeply than any one of us ever could on his own. Indeed, one of the things we deplore is the shallowness of so much deploring today. It is frankly deplorable that, with the world in the state it is, deploring has so signally failed to rise to the occasion by sinking to the new depths which are only waiting to be plumbed.

It is surely economic madness, at a time when the communications industry is increasingly dominated by large multinational corporations, to leave letter-writing to the backyard efforts of individual correspondents. We believe that no Letter to the Editor should be accepted for publication in this day and age unless it is signed by at least twenty people, of whom half should have some kind of titles or letters after their name. Indeed, as the advent of the fax and E-mail make it ever easier to circulate drafts of proposed letters among ever wider circles of possible signatories, we look forward to lists of signatures numbered not in tens but in thousands.

We are a curious nation. We complain about the over-crowding of our letters columns – but we continue to allow precious column-inches to be taken up by letters selfishly occupied by only one signatory. No wonder our forests are being laid waste to provide writing paper. No wonder carbon dioxide emissions are soaring, as readers light bonfires with newspapers which they have so little personal motivation to preserve.

We should perhaps add that this letter would also have been signed by Tessa Tilling MA PhD FRZS, only she wanted to insist on adding a paragraph about animal rights, whereupon Lord Blastwater, who has financial interests in this area, threatened to withdraw, together with some thirty business colleagues. This, we should explain, is a minority paragraph signed by †Twicester MA DD and (Mrs) Cynthia Treadwell CBE in protest.

In the light of this, may we urge? We should certainly hope we may. Or is this fundamental right to be taken away from us, like so many others, by unelected quangos and faceless bureaucrats in Brussels? If we, who between us have so much experience in urging, are not to be allowed to urge, then what hope is there for freedom of urging in this country?

We therefore call upon the Government. We call upon them daily, but we are never invited in. This is further evidence, if evidence be needed, of the national decline in good manners. We do not expect to be offered lunch, but surely it is not too much to hope for a cup of tea or coffee? It cannot be beyond the wit of man to provide a simple cup of something, together perhaps with cake or biscuits, for 270 tired and hungry letter-writers (or 271, should Renforth Ossett BA MBE surface at the prospect of free refreshments). If the Government should ever take it into its head to call upon us in return, they will find our door open – indeed, all 270 (or 271) of our doors.

We feel we must at this point sound a note of warning. In our concern for the mass letter-writing market we must not forget the plight of single letter-writers. We should in all fairness make clear that this is a further minority paragraph signed by †Twicester MA DD and (Mrs) Cynthia Treadwell CBE.

What nonsense! We personally feel – and this is the vast majority of us writing now – that quite enough concern has been expressed already for so-called 'single letter-writers'. If they didn't want to be single letter-writers, why didn't they make the simple effort to meet other letter-writers with similar outlooks, as the rest of us have, and set up happy, loving letters together? Every view, in our humble opinion, needs at least two authors to cherish it.

Not in *our* even more humble opinion.

Who wrote that last paragraph? Is this †Twicester MA DD and (Mrs) Cynthia Treadwell CBE breaking ranks once again? It would be helpful if signatories wishing to make some personal comment would identify themselves.

Oh, yes, sorry – (Lady) Frances Huffey CVO and (Sir) Rufus Tort QC and for that matter DSO, though I don't usually mention this in informal contexts.

May we say how much we agree with Lady Huffey and Sir Rufus Tort? And this expression of support, we are not ashamed to say, *does* come from †Twicester MA DD and (Mrs) Cynthia Treadwell CBE. We utterly reject the attempts being made by the big battalions of signatories to suppress the views of minorities amongst us. We can only applaud the sentiments that Lady Huffey and Sir Rufus express about paragraph ten.

May I say (Blastwater, Chairman, Associated Swill Industries), with respect, through the letterhead, that

100

†Twicester and (Mrs) Cynthia Treadwell, for all their display of doctorates and orders, are exactly the kind of perpetually cavilling, sententious, hand-wringing whingers who get the rest of us a bad name, or names?

I for one (D. P. Snedding, Deputy-Chairman, Associated Swill Industries) heartily agree with Lord Blastwater.

I for two – B. B. Brumfit, Director of Public Affairs, Associated Swill Industries – would like to know why (Mrs) Treadwell keeps her marital status so carefully wrapped in brackets? Does she view being married as a source of shame? Why for that matter is (Mr) Treadwell not in evidence? Does he not see eye-to-eye with his wife? I should also be interested to hear the views of †Twicester's good lady on her husband's choice of co-signatory.

May I say – and I speak as one who is Charles G. Strumley MD FRCS – in defence of †Twicester MA DD and (Mrs) Cynthia Treadwell CBE, that they are being unnecessarily modest when they say that they 'can only applaud the sentiments' of Lady Huffey and Sir Rufus. To my personal knowledge they can also dance an elegant foxtrot together, as they demonstrated most notably at the last annual get-together of signatories.

Some of us (Grace Threadneedle and others) would prefer to leave personalities aside and get back to the urgent questions facing us all in the world today. First and foremost of these is surely whether paragraph nine of this letter should be allowed to stand in its present form.

If paragraph nine goes (Professor Sir Thirlmere Stagg MA PhD and others) then so do all of us in the Paragraph Nine Support Group!

What some of us (B. B. Brumfit, and all in Associated Swill Industries) want to know is why nothing has been

101

heard of from †Twicester MA DD and (Mrs) Cynthia Treadwell CBE for several paragraphs now. So far as we can see from here their names are no longer in the list of signatories below. Have they perhaps run off together so as to be entirely alone in thinking?

We remain,
Yours, etc.

CRAWFORD ('BILL') STRIVE
MRS CRAWFORD ('BUBU') STRIVE
CRAWFORD STRIVE II (aged 5)
VICTORIA CRAWFORD STRIVE (aged 2 years 5½ months)
GRANDFATHER STRIVE (aged 93)
THE STRIVES' NANNY (aged 22)
MUSWELL TRACTION, a friend and neighbour of the Strives (aged 41, if this is relevant)
MRS MUSWELL TRACTION (also aged 41, though my birthday in fact falls three months after my husband's!)
'DISGUSTED' (age withheld)
(MRS) 'DISGUSTED'
'SICKENED' (aka 'FORMER SPURS SUPPORTER')
'OUTRAGED' (née 'DOG LOVER')
'NOT AMUSED' (LORD)
'MILDLY AMUSED' (THE HONOURABLE MISS)
ALL THE LADS AT THE JOLLY WATCHMAKERS
Etc.

Sandra Sesame

You have dealings from time to time with various large and complex organisations – international corporations, professional bodies, public authorities. You're a humble private citizen, and your business with them is modest.

You ring them to get one replacement part, one small piece of information, one minor adjustment to your account. They are publishing your thesis on Carolingian funeral customs, perhaps, or manufacturing some little range of armaments you've designed. You have never set foot inside their doors, but you know that at the other end of the line are dozens, hundreds, thousands of people, organised into departments and divisions, structured into grades and hierarchies, in ways that are completely opaque to you and the rest of the outside world.

'How can I help you?' asks the impersonal corporate voice that answers their phone. What do you say? How *can* it help you? How do you, in your lowly state of singleness and ignorance, enter into communication with this mighty complex of manifold unknowability?

Well, you have a magic formula. Two simple words.

'Sandra Sprott,' you tell the corporate voice authoritatively.

How did you first get hold of this name? You can't remember. Someone you met at a party told you. Or the first time you rang the organisation they put you through to various people with various names and positions, who put you through to various other people, with various other names and positions, and the one name you somehow caught was Sandra Sprott, though you never quite understood what it was she actually did. You wrote it down on the back of an envelope nevertheless, and somehow the envelope was still lying on your desk the next time you had to call them. So you asked for Sandra Sprott, and Sandra Sprott seemed to have a dim recollection of dealing with you before. On this fragile basis you have built some kind of continuing human relationship.

You still don't know what she does, even so, or very much else about her, except her name. You know that she once told you how to fill in a GX/33/Y (Exemption) form, and that raises some faint hope that this time she will also be able to help you get the washing-machine repaired, or obtain tickets for the opera.

Or possibly not. You may be asking her to do things which are not part of her professional responsibility at all, since you have so little idea what her professional responsibility is. *She* knows that applications for exemption go to Documentation, and exemptions from documentation go to Applications – but *not* to Lynette Swordsmith, who only deals with Overseas, except in the absence of Peter Cork, who is also responsible for Foreign (not to be confused with Overseas!), and certainly *not* to Elwyn Eady, who is notoriously difficult about such things – probably not even to the ever-reliable Jane, in Ted Thorough's office, since she is moving next week to run the vehicle fleet in the Devotional Software Division.

Nothing of this is vouchsafed to you, though. So of course you worry about your helpless dependence upon Ms Sprott. Are you embarrassing her by asking her to do things which are beyond her, or beneath her? Is she coping with you merely out of the goodness of her heart? Are you her private welfare case?

Probably when you first got put through to her it was because she was so junior that she was the person to

104

whom everyone who didn't know anyone in the organisation got put through. She was so humble that she didn't like to tell you you'd got the wrong department altogether, so raw that she didn't even realise herself. Maybe she's nothing to do with the publication of academic theses – she's in the Industrial Paints Division. To get your awful thesis published she had to get on to someone *she* knows in the Trade Directories and Gazetteers section, and get them to do a favour for *her*, even though they're obviously not the right person, either – it's just that they've *always* done favours for her, and they don't like to start saying no now that they've become a Deputy Controller.

And of course she's been promoted herself since the far-off day when you established that first tremulous contact. She's now *Director* of the Industrial Paints Division. She's sitting there trying to think large strategic thoughts about expansion in the Pacific Basin and downsizing in the North Sea, and there's this idiot on the line who wants to make a correction to a footnote on eighth-century shroud-weaving techniques.

You're not to know this, of course. But there's something about her voice that makes you suspect. Every time you ring her you apologise at length for wasting her time – and waste minutes more of it in the process.

All this is bad enough, for a sensitive person like yourself. But then something even worse happens. A terrible day comes when you phone, and she's not there. She's left the organisation. Probably she made a mess of the Pacific Basin expansion programme, thanks to perpetual distractions and interruptions. Your magic formula no longer works. Your pass has been cancelled, your thread into the labyrinth has snapped.

You get put through instead to someone whose name you don't catch. You tell them your name. They don't

105

catch it. You explain what you want. They sigh. You ask them humbly who else you should speak to. They don't know. You are out in the cold again.

And now your phone's ringing, and there's someone called Sandra Sprott on the line for you. 'I'm terribly sorry to bother you – I know how busy you must be.' You *are* very busy, it's true, but you don't like to say so because there's something vaguely familiar about the name – you have a feeling that she may be the relative of a friend, or the friend of a relative. 'No, no,' you lie, and you have to wait while she wastes yet more time on expressions of gratitude before she explains that her children are doing a project at school on the Industrial Revolution, and that she remembered your name because you were something to do with history . . .

Eternity in a tube of toothpaste

The lotos-eaters, in Tennyson's poem, live in a land where it seems always afternoon. Tennyson reports no complaints from them about this arrangement, and Odysseus's men, as soon as they have eaten a little of the fruit themselves, decide they are perfectly happy to settle down here as well, and give up all prospect of morning, evening, or night.

Permanent afternoon would have its drawbacks, of course. It would be sad if one never got to teatime, tragic if dinner remained forever beyond the horizon. But at least it's better getting stuck in the afternoon than where all the rest of us are stuck – in the morning. And in one particular bit of the morning, at that. Not breakfast-time, or coffee-break, or the approaches to lunch. In the land of the Gala apple-eaters, where you and I live, it's always getting-up time.

Have you noticed this? I mean that whenever you become conscious of the time, that's when it is. Whenever you think about what you are actually doing at this particular moment in time, what you're doing is cleaning your teeth. You're looking at yourself in the mirror and you're thinking, Here I am again, cleaning my teeth. And you're thinking that this is a pretty dreary thing to be doing. You're also thinking that the last thing before this that you can remember being actually conscious of doing was looking at yourself in the mirror as you cleaned your teeth the previous morning.

You remember what you were thinking as you did it,

too. You were thinking, Here I am again, cleaning my teeth. And you were thinking that this was a pretty dreary thing to be doing. You were also thinking that the last thing before this that you could remember being actually conscious of doing was looking at yourself in the mirror as you cleaned your teeth the *previous* morning. Etcetera. It's as if there were another mirror behind you as well, and you could see your life stretching away in both directions into glass-green infinity. And what are you doing in each increasingly remote green moment of this infinity? You're cleaning your teeth.

No, there is some variation. For men, at any rate, it's sometimes a slightly different time. It's a few minutes later, when they're shaving, and things are even drearier than they were when they were cleaning their teeth. Or, worse, in my case – it's a few minutes earlier, when I'm lying in bed trying to decide whether I should get up and *start* brushing my teeth and shaving. I'm trying to decide whether to get up precisely *now*, or whether I could safely leave it an instant longer, and get up say . . . now. Or . . . now . . . Then worrying that if I don't get up *now*, which is where it's got to now . . . or even *now* . . . then it's difficult to see how I'm ever going to get up at all, so that the dreary prospect of looking in the mirror and all the rest of it is always going to be in front of me, which is even worse than its actually happening.

You're vaguely aware at these moments that other things have somehow been going on in your life as well as getting up, though it's difficult to know when you managed to fit them in. Some of these things, you dimly recall, were more agreeable than this, others were even less. But they were notably agreeable or disagreeable enough – notably *notable* enough – for you to be conscious only of the things themselves, and not of yourself experiencing them.

108

A lot of perfectly ordinary things have happened, for that matter. You had lunch the previous day, you walked down the street, you felt a cold coming on. But they were so ordinary that you were scarcely conscious of them at all. You weren't looking in the mirror at the time, of course. This probably helped.

But the last time you were actually thinking about what you were doing, you were getting up. So your life, as something that you are actually conscious of, rather than something that's just rushing past without your quite being able to take it in, has closed up into one long, continuous, extremely dreary moment of getting up. It's Wednesday, and it's time to get up. It's Monday, and it's time to get up. It's November 13th, 1959, and it's time to get up. It's January 19th, 1995, and it's time to get up . . .

One day somebody is doing to be writing your biography. Is it going to appeal to a wide readership, this biography of yours? I believe it's not. I believe your biography is headed straight for the remainders table.

This is obviously what eternity is going to be like. Today, and time to get up . . . Still today, and time to get up . . .

I understand this kind of thing happens to space travellers in science-fiction stories – they get stuck in time-warps. They presumably manage to extract themselves and struggle back to earth with the help of various pieces of implausible science and fictitious mathematics. How are we ever going to get out of ours, with nothing but a toothbrush and a razor strangely encrusted with solidified shaving cream?

Actually it's not just space-travellers who get trapped in time-warps. It's always happening, in the most respectable kind of books. But they're stuck in the past in some kind of way, which might be more interesting.

109

They've reverted to their childhood, or they're still living in some rather memorable moment of triumph or disaster. It wouldn't be much fun to spend your entire life watching the rats running over the cobwebbed ruins of your wedding-cake, I see that. But it would surely be more interesting than spending it cleaning your teeth, or shaving the lefthand side of your face.

People are always recommending living in the present, it's true. But couldn't it at least be a different present? Couldn't it be breakfast time? Yes, why doesn't one get stuck in breakfast time, which comes round just as often as shaving? Why couldn't it happen that every time one notices what one's doing it turns out to be drinking delicious fresh orange juice, with the morning paper propped up against the coffeepot, full of appetising fresh catastrophes? Perhaps if one fixed up a mirror on the breakfast table . . .?

After all, the lotos-eaters never seemed to have cleaned their teeth at all. Maybe their teeth fell out before they were thirty. Are they worrying about this? Apparently not.

How *do* you get out of the warp? You never discover. One moment you've been cleaning your teeth since the beginning of time, and you're going to go on cleaning them until the end of time, at which point, if Stephen Hawking is right, you'll start cleaning them backwards, and go on cleaning them backwards until you get back to the Big Bang, when you'll start cleaning them forwards again . . . Then somehow, miraculously, you've broken through to breakfast time, and orange juice and economic crises are going on around you.

But scarcely have you got on to your second cup of coffee when out of nowhere it's tomorrow, and it's time to get up.

Gentle reader

Chapter One

The old man's head lolled helplessly from side to side like a rag-doll's as Zack heaved him up off the bed. 'What are you doing?' cried Precious. 'He needs some air,' grunted Zack, as he half-carried, half-dragged the inert fat body across to the open window. He propped it in the window-frame for a moment and looked out. They were ten floors up. It was difficult to estimate how big an area the old man would spread over . . .

I know what you're doing, incidentally. You. Yes, *you*! I, the author, know what you, the reader, are doing. You think I have the imagination and insight to understand what's going on inside the dark, twisted souls of Zack and Precious, and I don't know what some simple citizen like *you* is up to?

You're standing in the bookshop, and you're flicking through the first page or two of this novel, trying to decide whether to buy it or not. You're worried that a whole paragraph has gone by already, and so far not a sign of anyone having even the most mundane form of sexual intercourse. Look, be reasonable. One thing at a time. How can they have intercourse when he's trying to push her old father out of the window?

If they gave him a really good shove, thought Zack, he might fall slightly wide of the building, and hit one or two of the winos lying stretched out on the pavement . . .

Also, you're trying to remember whether you read anything in the paper about my getting some huge advance. It would help you to believe that this novel was worth £14.99 if you knew that the publishers had paid out a little more than £14.99 on it themselves.

In fact you're starting to worry about the whole level of the publishers' commitment to this enterprise. You're very suspicious because the book wasn't in a dump-bin, stacked fifty copies high. There was no showcard in the window. You're not even sure there's an author tour, with readings and signings in selected bookshops, and wide media coverage.

Look, come on. We're not discussing your life's savings. We're talking about an investment of £14.99. Of which I get 10%. That's what you'll be paying me. Because let's get this absolutely straight. We're going to be examining with ruthless honesty the relationship between Zack and Precious, so let's start off by getting *our* relationship clear. It's written down here in my contract, look, signed and countersigned. 'A royalty of 10% on the first 2,500 copies.' That's the total extent of the emotional demand I am making upon you – a fraction of a penny under £1.50. All right? Just go over to the cash-desk and get your credit card out.

On the other hand, there was a noticeable cross-wind blowing, which might carry the body a little off course, and deposit it on top of the kids sniffing glue behind the rubbish-bins ...

What, you're still hesitating? Look, I'd like to give it to you for a pound – I'd like to make you a present of it. No, that's not true, I wouldn't. Not because I care about the money, but because I don't think that would be a true or healthy relationship between us. We're trying to start a business connection, not a love-affair. The cash-desk. Over there by the door, look.

Suddenly the old man uttered a terrible groan. 'He's still alive,' said Precious. Zack gave up trying to work out the exact point of impact, and began to ease the body out into space. He didn't want to rush something like this, but he also didn't want any further discussion with the old man about a European currency . . .

No? You think this is exploitation, £1.50? How far can you go in a cab for £1.50? For £1.50 with me you can go all the way from the dark heart of the urban jungle in Balham to the glittering high life of newly-rich derivatives traders in Barnet. And you don't end up as a slippery pulp spread across a major traffic intersection in West Norwood, like Zack on page 397, causing a busload of orphans to run into a truck carrying weapons-grade plutonium. You don't get secretly dumped from a sludge-carrier in the North Sea, entombed in fifteen separate concrete nuclear-waste containers, as part of a global hush-up involving the White House and the Vatican.

You arrive home on page 463, shaken and seared, but fit and well, sitting in your own armchair with a glass of lightly chilled chardonnay in your hand and a bowl of taco chips in front of you. For £1.50! No hidden extras. No airport tax, no gratuities to guides. You buy the wine and the taco chips, the rest's on me. I think you have a pretty good deal.

Or maybe you're not one of those first 2,500 pioneers who rushed to the bookshops as soon as stocks arrived. Maybe you're one of the readers numbered 2,501 to 5,000, from whom my contract stipulates that I get 12.5%. All right, so we have a slightly different relationship. We have a £1.87375 relationship. How do we feel about this? I'll tell you how *I* feel about it. I feel good about it. I feel

I'm selling you something that people want to buy. I believe you feel good, too. You think, OK, so I'm paying a little over the odds for this, but that's the kind of person I am – someone who's ready to pay a premium price for a premium product. This is the kind of novel that 2,500 people have bought already. This novel is beginning to be hot. Hot costs.

Unless you're the 5,001st customer – unless you're one of the people who are paying me 15% thereafter. You see me getting my hands on a cool £2.2485 of your money, and you feel you're being taken for a ride. Well, why not? I mean, frankly. You're a Johnny-come-lately. You should have run down to the bookshop along with my fashion-conscious friends 2,501 to 5,000, as soon as they saw it lying on the coffee-tables of their innovative neighbours 1 to 2,500.

Or did you by any chance pick this up off the remainders table? Because if you did I'm getting nothing at all. You know what I think of a reader like you? I despise you. You're cheap. You get to the scene where they torture Precious to death with an electric toothbrush, you'll have a heart-attack, you'll die.

Get out of the shop! Go home! You think I'm going to give you bizarre forms of intercourse and violence for nothing? This is what you get for nothing:

Zack grabbed the old man by the ankles as he fell, and with a huge effort hauled him back into the window. 'Sorry,' he said. 'Just kidding.'

And they all sat down together and had a good laugh and a nice cup of tea.

Money well changed

No more Wechsel. The last of the summer Cambio. The real sadness of the Single European Currency is that it would mean the end of European moneychanging as we know it.

I recall many delightfully unhurried exchanges of currency and traveller's cheques all over Europe, many delicious stews of noughts and decimal points, many entertaining failures to have my passport with me or to remember that banks close for lunch. But if I had to select just one occasion to recall in the bleak years ahead it would be a certain Monday morning in late June at the Banque de France in Laon.

Laon, appropriately enough, is at the crossroads of Europe. It's in the Aisne, in Northern France, situated just off the motorway that runs from Strasbourg and Germany to the French Channel ports, at the point where it crosses the N2 from Paris to Brussels. Whichever road you're on you can see it coming from miles off – two ancient Gothic cathedral towers perched on a fortified hilltop islanded in the great agricultural plain. Two stars in the Michelin – three for the nave of the cathedral – wonderful views.

This charming town was full of sunshine and the bustle of market day when we found ourselves in need of a little financial refreshment there. We were on our way back from South Germany, and we needed a little more French currency to see us through to Calais. We had it in mind to change some forty pounds' worth of left-over German marks, together with a £20 sterling traveller's cheque. The Banque de France seemed like a good choice for our custom. Its appearance was discreetly imposing, its name suggested solidity and extensive reserves. We were right. The feast of fine banking that ensued was worth another three stars in the Michelin. I was so impressed that I made a complete note of it, course by course, from the moment we pressed the yellow button beside the heavily-armoured front door.

1 A red light comes on to indicate that our application for entry is being considered. We are instructed to wait for a green light before attempting to push the door.
2 The green light comes on, and we enter, to be confronted by a second door, with a second yellow button. A second red light comes on, while our credentials are examined all over again.
3 We pass through the second door, and enter a great hall divided by a counter. On the other side of the counter are a dozen or so employees of the bank. On this side is a spacious emptiness occupied only by us. We are the only people in Laon to have passed both tests.
4 We advance towards the counter and the waiting staff. We choose the nearest clerk, on the righthand side of the bank, and present our £20 traveller's cheque, our passport, and our 130 Deutschmarks. The clerk examines the cheque. She examines the passport, then takes a printed form and writes down by hand the number of the passport, together with my name and address. She examines the fifty-Deutschmark note, then the three twenties, then the ten and the two fives. She goes away to consult the bank's files.

5 She comes back and performs various computations upon a small pocket calculator. The calculator is for some reason balanced half on and half off a ledger, so that it gives to the touch like a pudding. She writes down by hand on the printed form the quantities of sterling and Deutschmarks involved, the rates for each currency, and the two subtotals in francs. She performs another wobbly computation, and writes down the total. So far, a dignified but not unusual display of traditional handcraft moneychanging.

6 But this is merely the *amuse-gueule* before the meal proper. The clerk takes the form she has filled up, together with the passport, the traveller's cheque, and the seven Deutschmark bills, to a more senior-looking woman, who has drawnback grey hair and steel-rimmed spectacles. She checks the two multiplications and the addition. She re-examines the passport, the traveller's cheque, and the German banknotes, and returns them to the clerk. Everything is in order. The clerk returns to the counter and hands us back our passport. She retains the traveller's cheque – but she hands back our Deutschmarks. What?

7 She indicates a male cashier in a small fortified enclosure a kilometre or two away on the lefthand side of the great hall. Of course. A division of functions familiar from many such occasions in the past.

8 We walk across to the cashier. The clerk, on the other side of the counter, also walks across to the cashier. *We* are holding the passport and the returned DM 130; *she* is holding the £20 traveller's cheque and the form she has filled up, as checked and authenticated by her senior. We wait for the cashier

117

to take the Deutschmarks through the front of the security grille; she waits for the cashier to open a special window in the back of it and take the traveller's cheque and the form.

9 The clerk returns to her post on the righthand side of the bank.

10 The cashier examines the traveller's cheque once again, then consults another set of files. He reworks the computations on the completed form. He takes the seven Deutschmark bills from us, and examines them again in their turn – first the fifty, then the three twenties, then the ten and the two fives. They all apparently pass muster once again. Nothing has changed, in this rapidly changing world, since they were first examined and re-examined on the righthand side of the bank.

11 Or has it? The cashier is evidently shaken by a sudden doubt. How about the exchange rates? Some fair amount of time has now gone by since they were checked and double-checked on the other side of the bank. There may have been dramatic developments in the markets since then. The Federal Government may have fallen. The pound may be soaring even as the Deutschmark goes into free fall. He looks up both the rates again. Nothing has happened. Pound and mark alike are rock steady.

12 This steadiness in the markets makes a pleasing contrast with the cashier's pocket calculator, which is balanced half on and half off a ledger, just like the clerk's, so that it gives like a second helping of pudding as he punches each button, and recomputes all the computations that he has just reworked manually.

13 There is evidently something a little unsettling

about the result of this fourth trip through the sums. I suspect the trouble is that the new results are *exactly the same* as the earlier ones, which may of course tend to confirm them, but which may on the other hand suggest the possibility of systematic error in the bank's methodology for multiplication and addition. The cashier summons a second cashier, who goes through all the rates and calculations for a fifth time. I notice that he too keeps the calculator balanced half on and half off the ledger as he works. Sponge *calculatrice* is obviously a *specialité de la maison*.

14 And yes – steps are being taken. Action is in hand. The first cashier has let himself out of his cage. He is walking all the way back across the bank towards the righthand side. We cross back as well, separated from him by the counter, in parallel, anxious to stay in touch with events. I believe he is carrying the traveller's cheques and the German banknotes, but he evidently doesn't have everything with him, because after he has spoken to the clerk on the righthand side she leaves her position, and we all walk back again to the lefthand side.

15 I'm not sure that it's the correctness of the mathematics that are at issue now – the calculator has been left to one side. I have the impression that they have moved on to more general questions. After all, not two but three different currencies are involved in this transaction, and there may be problems of protocol and precedence. Should the Bundesbank or the Bank of England be informed first?

16 A long time goes by. It is very quiet and still inside the bank, and my attention wanders. I find myself

covertly watching some of the other staff. I become fascinated by one particular man. He is recklessly handsome, with a moustache and a three-piece suit, and he has nothing at all to do. The desk in front of him is completely empty. He rubs his hands together and gazes into space, with a look of wistful tenderness. I don't believe he is thinking about high-interest savings accounts, or even ways of making the bank's foreign exchange procedures more secure. I believe he is thinking about some member of the opposite sex.

17 I notice that there is in fact a young woman sitting just in front of him, typing rapidly, until there is nothing more to type, when she, too, leans on her empty desk and gazes into the great spaces of the room. I believe her thoughts have also strayed back to her private life. They do not talk to each other. They do not look at each other. I get the impression that it's not each other that they are thinking about. Their separate reveries seem strangely deep and poignant in the quiet lofty room.

18 Just a moment. Something's happened . . . I don't know what it was, but the clerk is walking back to her place on the righthand side of the bank. It's been settled. Everyone's anxieties over the transaction have been set to rest.

19 The clerk fills out a second form to replace the first one.

20 She walks back to the cashier with the new edition of the form. I have the impression that she is moving a little more slowly than before. Her footwear, I think, is not entirely suitable for active pursuits like currency exchange.

21 The cashier checks the new figures and the current

state of the foreign exchange market. He pays over Fr. 636.27.

22 We exit through the double security system.

The sun is still shining. We are in no hurry, and Laon is a delightful place to be. I look at my watch; the whole entertainment has taken twenty-five minutes.

So what's going to happen to everyone in the Banque de France in Laon when the ecu comes? How are the rest of us going to fill our time? We're *all* going to end up staring into space, thinking about our loved ones.

The Magic Mobile

When the curtain rises on Act Two of my opera *The Magic Mobile* the scene is set in the Check-In Hall of a major international Airport.

Solemn Muzak is heard, and Sarastro, the Airport Manager, enters. He informs the assembled Staff that a Traveller is approaching the doors of the Airport, seeking admission to their Mysteries. The Traveller, he tells them, wishes to throw off everything that shackles him to the Earth below, and ascend towards the Light and Purity of Heaven.

The Airport Staff remind the Manager that in a major international Airport this Goal can be reached only through diligence and suffering, and they question whether the Traveller will be able to endure the process. The Manager tells them to perform their sacred office, and to test the Traveller's resolve by a series of rituals and tests, so that he progresses towards his symbolic Enlightenment only by gradual stages.

The glass doors now slide back, and the Traveller, Papageno, enters. He is carrying a Mobile Phone, and as he hurries distractedly towards the Ticket Desk, which is the first stage of his Ordeal, he is playing a cheerful little tune upon its musical buttons. He is ringing his partner, Papagena, and explaining to her in a dramatically charged aria ('You're not going to believe this, but') that in Act One he had to leave home in too much of a hurry to use public transport, as he had planned, and that he has been forced to take the car instead, which he knows she is shortly going to be needing herself, for some spiritual odyssey of her own.

But before Papagena in reply has had time to develop her feelings about this musically, Papageno is undergoing his first ritual purification at the hands of the Ticket Staff. In a short cavatina ('The flight is heavily') the Sales Person makes a preliminary assessment of the Traveller's seriousness of purpose by declaring that there are now only Euro-Business seats available, at a substantial premium. After some earthily comic hesitation, Papageno expresses resignation to his fate, and is quietly relieved of a substantial proportion of his worldly wealth.

He is rewarded with a Passenger Ticket entitling him to proceed to the second stage of his Initiation at the Check-In Desk. The jaunty little theme for mobile phone is heard several times more, but before he can get through to Papagena and clarify their evidently now troubled relationship he has to present the Ticket, find his Passport, and answer a solemn ritual Interrogation about the Contents of his Suitcase. His answers proving satisfactory, the symbolically burdensome suitcase, and the various pieces of Electrical Apparatus he has confessed it contains, is spirited away, and his Passenger Ticket is returned, now accompanied by a Boarding Card marked with certain cabbalistic signs. Armed with Ticket, Passport, and Boarding Card, he proceeds to the Bank to acquire Currency suitable for the world he is hoping to reach. Again and again the Mobile Phone theme is heard, until he is at last able to explain with breathless haste to Papagena in the prestissimo 'Listen, listen, listen' that he is going to post the Parking Ticket to her, so that she can come down to the Airport at her leisure and collect the car.

His relations with Papagena seem to be still in a somewhat equivocal state as he runs back and forth trying to find where to buy an Envelope and a Stamp, and then hastens to the barrier of the Inner Sanctuary, beyond which only Postulants holding a Boarding Card are admitted. Papageno is indeed, as we know, holding the precious Boarding Card, but since he is also holding the Passenger Ticket, the Passport, the Foreign Currency, the Parking Ticket, the Envelope and the Stamp he has the opportunity for further comic business, accompanied by the delightfully desperate 'I know I had it when' before he is allowed to proceed, and is consequently in a state of some confusion at his next Ordeal in Security Control, as the Body Scanner plays the ominous Body Scanner theme, and he is forced to empty his pockets of the Mobile Phone, his Pocket Calculator, his Keys, and his remaining Small Change.

It only remains for him to have his Passport checked once again in Passport Control before he is rewarded by admission to the manifold delights of the Departure Lounge. Here he is offered food and drink, and gratefully accepts a Takeaway Coffee and a Freshly Baked Croissant, since he missed breakfast, before he hastens to purchase a small phial of Duty-Free Perfume to enclose with the Parking Ticket in the hope of rescuing his threatened relationship with Papagena. Sarastro and the secretly watching Security Men almost give up hope for Papageno when he seems tempted by some of the other earthly goods on offer, and for a moment contemplates purchasing a duty-free 48-inch television with quadrophonic speakers, which they doubt can ever be got airborne. But he is saved by the disembodied voice of the Queen of Flight singing the famous coloratura aria 'This is the final call for passengers on'.

He now enters the most arduous stage of his Initiation – the long walk to Gate 73, checking as he goes that he still has the Passenger Ticket, the Passport, the Boarding

Card, the Foreign Currency, the Parking Ticket, the Envelope, the Stamp, the Pocket Calculator, the Keys, the Small Change, the Takeaway Coffee, the Freshly Baked Croissant, and the Perfume. Many times he almost forgets where he is going. Many times he is tempted to settle for Gate 35 and Helsinki, or Gate 51 and Philadelphia. All that drives him on is the need to find somewhere to sit down for a moment and lighten his burden by putting the Passenger Ticket in the Envelope, and the Parking Ticket in the back of the Passport, after which he will need only a Rubbish Bin where he can post the Envelope, and a Post Box where he can dump the greasy remains of the Croissant.

A trio of smiling sopranos greets him as he at last totters up to Gate 73. 'Boarding Card and Passport,' they brightly sing. As he spreads all his possessions out over the floor to locate them once again, they inform him that the nearest Post Box is in the Check-In Hall – part of a profane world that has long since closed behind him forever.

He stumbles on into the Final Departure Lounge. He has one last chance to phone Papagena and try to explain what has happened before the use of Mobile Phones is forbidden during the heavenward Ascent. His fingers form the familiar jaunty pattern on the buttons. But, in a musical master-stroke of heart-breaking poignancy, all we hear is silence. There are no buttons for him to play upon, because he has left the Mobile Phone lying on the table at Security Control.

Only now is he sufficiently chastened to enter the winding narrow corridor that leads to the ultimate Goal of his Ordeal. He bows his head abjectly to pass through the last low doorway – and when he raises it again he is in a new and better world, with heavenly Muzak playing, and the Cabin Crew welcoming him in the joyous finale,

'Thank you for choosing'. They hope he has a pleasant flight, they sing, as the triumphant clunking of Seat-Belts is heard and the curtain falls.

So now all our victorious hero has to face is Act Three, and Disenlightenment at the other end.

Unbind their feet

Football and news about football currently occupies not much more than seventy per cent of the space in newspapers and the time on television. Whole days occasionally pass with no mention of the game in the main headlines.

Football-lovers feel that it would represent a truer reflection of people's interests if this figure were closer to a hundred per cent. Is the game's present poor showing the result of anti-football prejudice in the media? Or is it – as unprejudiced observers increasingly believe – because of the pettifogging restrictions under which the game labours?

Everyone knows that keeping football in the news calls for a sustained and wholehearted effort by players and supporters alike to maintain the levels of violence and corruption required in today's highly competitive markets. Why then do so few goalkeepers seem prepared to accept bribes to let in goals? Why are referees and managers mostly so resistant to flexible modern business ethics? More important still, perhaps – why are players not more eager to assault each other with their full natural vigour? Why do so many matches go by without any real effort by the spectators to cause a reasonable level of physical injury, damage to property, and international ill-feeling?

The answer, we believe at the Genghis Khan Institute, the independent think-tank where I and so many other famous thinkers do our thinking, is obvious. It's because

127

initiative in all these areas is punished instead of being rewarded. The game is enmeshed in a web of outdated rules, archaic laws, and fuddy-duddy statutes. Naturally players are reluctant to co-operate with go-ahead entrepreneurs in the gambling industry if next thing they know they're going to be hauled up in front of some inquisitor for their pains. Naturally it's going to discourage people from kicking someone's face in, or setting fire to the stadium, if it's merely going to result in answering time-wasting questions from some officious constable.

In other words, the football industry is ripe for deregulation. The deregulation of institutions such as the Stock Exchange and Lloyds has shown what can be done in setting people's initiative free – the exploits of deregulated bankers, dealers, and underwriters have really seized the public's imagination. Indeed, at the Genghis Khan Institute we feel that interest in their doings has now gone a little too far. They need to be allowed to get on with their work out of the limelight – which is an added reason for trying to divert the public's attention to healthy outdoor sports.

The first stage in rolling back the nanny state, we believe, is to decriminalise bribery. Everyone enjoys giving or taking an occasional bribe. Everyone knows how useful bribes are in breaking the ice, and making business relationships go with a swing, so let's stop being hypocritical about it.

Then let's sweep away all namby-pamby restrictions on violence. The sight of spectators hurling impotent abuse at players from the stands, accompanied perhaps by coins and bananas, is a sorry one. We want to see the fans out there on the pitch, putting into effect any of their suggestions which are physiologically possible. Fast-food vendors in the vicinity of the ground should be encouraged to sell hand-grenades, and other simple personal

128

armaments. This would not only liven up the game, but provide a much-needed stimulus to the armaments industry and reduce unemployment by mopping up over-supply in the labour market.

Unthinkable? Of course. But then the *Titanic* was unsinkable!

And this is only a beginning. We need a bonfire of *all* the controls hampering the game. No one likes the official snoopers who run around blowing whistles and waving flags. Referees would soon be rationalised out of exist-ence if there were no rules to enforce; linesmen would very rapidly be looking for more profitable employment if there were no lines to patrol. Rules and lines, intro-duced into the game by successive Labour Governments, merely hamstring the players and slow the game down.

It was presumably also some band of whiskery Fabian do-gooders who decided what the goals of the game were supposed to be. Only vegetarians and socialists could think that any red-blooded man could ever settle for kicking a ball into some kind of glorified shrimping-net as his aim in life. Let's dump the goalposts in the skip where they belong, and pile each end of the pitch with bottles of beer, stacks of banknotes, and half-dressed girls.

Why do we need a pitch, though? All you need to play football is a foot and a ball! Confining the game inside arbitrary boundaries is entirely artificial. When this country was great, back in the Old Stone Age, was foot-ball played on fields? How could it have been? There were no fields! The game wandered freely over the whole face of the countryside, avoiding only private property, foxhunts, and military establishments. These apart, the players were entirely unrestricted until the whistle blew for time.

Except that the whistle *never* blew for time. Neither

whistles nor the concept of time had been invented! The game simply went on until there was no one left to play it! The use of a stone ball ensured a high turnover among the players, and encouraged new blood to come forward, often in spectacular quantities. Did anyone object? There is no record of it. The public realised that it reduced the burden of providing players with retirement pensions.

Football grounds, we believe, should be sold off to become shopping centres, or private hospitals to treat the injured. Some thinkers at the Institute even feel that it's difficult to justify the continued expense of providing a ball. Who wants to kick a ball when they can kick someone's head?

If we save money on the ball we can afford to pay internationally competitive rates to club directors. Then, under the cream of international management, we shall see British football, supported where necessary by the SAS and the threat of Trident missiles, overrunning at any rate some of the smaller European powers.

How, it may be asked, does all this fit in with the stern policies on law and order advocated in other studies published by the Genghis Khan Institute?

We can't think, for the life of us.

But if it's unthinkable then sooner or later we at the Institute will manage to think it. So stand by for another display of intellectual fireworks!

Ready, steady . . . no . . .

Now, have I got everything?

Shoulder-bag with my various bits and pieces in – yes, on my shoulder. I think that's all I need, isn't it? I'm only going to Tunbridge Wells. I'm only going to be away for two or three hours. Oh, keys, of course. . . . Not still lying on the hall table, are they, as has been known to happen occasionally in the past . . .? No, here in my hand, just where they ought to be.

Very satisfying. I do believe that for once I'm setting out in reasonably good time for something. I'm going to catch the train without any hurry at all.

So, just set the burglar-alarm, and I can . . .

Hold on. Better check I've got some money in my pocket . . . I did pick up my wallet . . .? Yes, I did. And my little organiser thing, and my penknife? I don't want to find myself in Tunbridge Wells for two hours without a penknife . . .

Yes, everything's under control . . . Oh, have I closed the bathroom window? Better look. Don't want to get halfway down the street and have to come running back . . . Yes, window closed. I did switch off the copier . . .? Oh, come on! Just set the burglar-alarm and . . . Ticket! Where's my ticket? I've forgotten my ticket!

No, here it is, neatly tucked away in the ticket section of my wallet. Perhaps I am finally beginning to get organised in life. Got my money, got my ticket, got my passport . . .

No, I haven't! I've forgotten my passport!

Now, don't be silly. Tunbridge Wells – remember? Tell the Tunbridge Wells Writers' Circle how to organise their professional lives, then home again. I don't need sun cream, I don't need a mosquito coil... Might need a spare sweater, though. I've no idea what the weather's doing down there in Kent. Might be pouring with rain... Rain, yes! Umbrella – where is it? And a comb. Gale blowing up Tunbridge Wells High Street – last few hairs seriously deranged. Not the kind of thing they like in Tunbridge Wells.

Anything else, before I definitively set the burglar-alarm? How about something to read on the train? Quick – look along the shelves – grab anything – haven't got all that much time now ... *The Brothers Karamazov* ... My God, it weighs a ton ...

Right – burglar-alarm on ... This departure has now taken slightly longer than the last act of *The Cherry Orchard*. Yes – I haven't left any aged retainers locked inside, have I? No, but I *am* leaving without a handkerchief! I was going to spend the entire talk wiping my nose on my sleeve!

Switch off the burglar alarm ... Take a spare handkerchief as well, perhaps. Driving rain coming under the umbrella – I might suddenly find I've got a cold coming on. Yes – better put some aspirin in ... And throat-lozenges ... What's this packet? Plasters ... Well, why not? Sensible precaution. Antiseptic cream, too. Pair of tweezers for getting splinters out ...

Spare socks? No, no, I'm not on a walking tour. Nice to have a map, though. And the map-measurer? Well ... why not ...? And the compass? Come on, this is getting out of hand ... Though since it takes up so little room ...

So ... This bag's going to burst. I'll just quickly transfer everything into a suitcase ...

Actually there's room for one or two more things, now I'm taking the suitcase. How about a few apples to eat on the train? We might break down between stations – get stuck overnight in a snowdrift ... Look round the kitchen as I collect the apples. That ball of string might come in handy. A few elastic bands ...

Right – burglar-alarm on and out of the door before I think of anything else! Double-lock the Yale. Lock the Chubb ... Only now I'm outside it feels distinctly warm. Supposing it turned out to be a heatwave? Better just run back in and take my vest off ...

Quick, quick – unlock the Chubb, unlock the Yale – switch off the burglar-alarm ... Coat off, shirt off, vest off – shirt on, coat on, alarm on ... On the other hand, ne'er cast a clout ... Alarm off, coat off, shirt off – vest on, shirt on, coat on, alarm on ... Stop! Where are the keys! I've put them down on the hall table, unbelievably. I'm going to lock myself out again! Grab keys – out of the door before the burglar-alarm goes off ... Lock Yale, lock Chubb. I'm going to have to hurry.

I can't hurry! Not with this load! Unlock, unlock. Alarm off. *Brothers Karamazov* out. Apples out. Spare handkerchief out. Elastic bands out ... Alarm on. Lock, lock. Now – *run*!

Run back! The talk! The text of my talk!

Unlock, unlock. Alarm off ... Where is it? Right ... Alarm on. Lock, lock. Run, run ...!

I did lock up ...? Back, back! Unlock Chubb – *was* locked – relock it. Unlock Yale – also locked – relock. Run! Except ... I never put the alarm on! Unlock, unlock. Beep beep ... I *did* put the alarm on! So – lock, lock. Run, run, run, run. ... SCREECH SCREECH!

What ...? Oh, my God, I never switched it *off*! Back, back! Fumble, fumble – SCREECH SCREECH! Fumble,

133

fumble, fumble – SCREECH, SCREECH, SCREECH! Fumble, fumble, fumble, fumble . . .

Finally restore peace. Reassure the neighbours. Put the keys and the suitcase very calmly and unhurriedly back on the hall table, and reassess the situation. OK, I've missed the train. Does that matter so very much, in the great scale of things? I'll get the next one! I simply ring Tunbridge Wells and tell them they'll have to talk quietly amongst themselves for an hour or two, sort out their own problems.

At least I've now got plenty of time to take a last look round . . . put the ball of string back in the kitchen, the plasters back in the medicine cabinet . . . take my vest off again . . . transfer the text of the talk and a few other bare essentials back into the shoulder-bag . . . put the shoulder-bag neatly back beside the keys on the hall table . . . turn on the burglar-alarm . . . and close the door behind me in unhurried dignity.

Shoulder-bag . . . I've left it on the hall table. Never mind – no rush now. Just quietly unlock the door and . . . Keys . . .! They're not . . .? They can't be . . .!

Our pleasure, Captain!

Good morning, ladies and gentlemen. My name's Thork, Peter Thork, I'm one of the passengers, I'm sitting in seat 33B . . .

Could we just have a bit of hush in the cabin . . .? A bit of hush, please . . .! Thank you. I haven't got a microphone, I'm afraid, unlike Captain Mellowdew! So I'll just have to shout. Can you hear me at the front? Can the cabin attendants hear me . . .? And Captain Mellowdew and his crew . . .?

Good. Right. Ladies and gentlemen – Captain Mellowdew and his crew – Director of Passenger Services Clake and his cabin staff – fellow-passengers . . . I won't keep you for long. I only want to say a few words in reply to the various very charming speeches we've heard from Mr Clake and Captain Mellowdew.

I have to fly quite a lot – I'm in international consultancy – and I sometimes can't help feeling a bit ashamed of the way we all just sit here and take the really kind and heartwarming speeches we always hear from the crew so much for granted. I thought that just for once someone ought to get up on his hind legs and say a word or two in reply.

So let me assure Mr Clake that we will indeed keep our seat-belts fastened when the sign is on, and that we won't smoke in the toilets. Thank you, Mr Clake, for your concern.

We were all, I think, particularly touched to be welcomed on board by Captain Mellowdew in person. We

135

know how busy he must be up there on the flight deck, and I think we all very much appreciated his finding a moment to talk to us. Particularly since he stressed that he was speaking not only for himself, but on behalf of all his crew, including his First Officer, Mr Timmins, and the Flight Engineer, Mr Huckle. I'd just like to say that we're very pleased to *be* here – and I know I'm speaking on behalf of at any rate Mr Ted Trice, in seat 33A beside me, and Mr G. T. Waddell in seat 33C.

Mr Clake, you'll remember, told us that he was being assisted by Cheryl and Shiree in the forward cabin, and by Lorraine, Fontana, Pearline, and Coralie in the aft cabin. I hope they'll forgive me if I've missed anyone out. Captain Mellowdew was kind enough to say that Mr Clake and his team would be doing their best to make our trip enjoyable. Let me assure him that their efforts are being highly successful, and that we are all enjoying ourselves hugely.

Captain Mellowdew – if I may address myself to you for a moment, if I may be personal – you said something else that particularly touched me. You thanked us for flying with you. I don't know about the others, but for some reason your words really touched a chord in me. I know how easy it is to take it for granted that people will get on your plane. I know how easy it is just to fly off without a word, get people to their destination, and never stop to appreciate their kindness in coming along. It means a lot to us, to know that the contribution we make on these occasions has been noted.

So let me tell you, Captain Mellowdew, very sincerely, what an honour it is for us to be able to play our part. We know things have been a little difficult for this airline in the past year, what with the record trading losses, and that slight mishap one of your planes had on touchdown at . . . well, on a happy occasion like this I don't want to

136

intrude upon what must be a very sensitive area. I'm confident, though, that when the report of the inquiry is published the blame will be put firmly on the local air-traffic control. And if we've been able to help just a little bit with the money side of things then it's all been worth while. What are passengers for, after all?

And, Captain Mellowdew, thank you so much for that very helpful information you gave us about the height we were flying at. I guessed it was 32,000 feet, Mr Trice thought 34,000. So when you told us it was in fact 33,000, we both felt our minds had been put at rest. Well worth being woken up for!

It occurs to me that you up there on the flight deck might like to know a little more about what's going on back here in the cabin. Well, some of us have been sleeping – or trying to! – and some of us have been reading or working. I couldn't help noting that Mr Trice was doing his expenses during the early part of the route, and that Mr Waddell has been wearing his headphones, lost in a world of his own. Mr Trice, I should perhaps tell you, informs me that he has a little back trouble, but I gather it's not too serious, and it's not expected to hold him up today.

So God bless you, Captain Mellowdew! And you, Mr Timmins and Mr Huckle! And you, Mr Clake, and you, Cheryl and Shiree in the forward cabin, together with Lorraine, Fontana, Pearline, and Coralie in the aft cabin! We won't forget you! We look forward to travelling with you again very soon. And I personally, now I've got started, look forward to the chance of letting you hear this very same speech, many, many more times in the future. Thank you.

Major minor

1 The press pack concerning the vision of Zebediah, the son of Ud.

2 Like unto rotten medlar fruits are the harlotries of Ashkelon, and the whoredoms of Moab cry unto heaven as the howling of wolves in the wilderness of Geshur. And the day shall come when the sons and daughters of Ashkelon are devoured by the cankerworm. In that day shall the fire of the Lord fall upon the husbandmen of Moab, and fry them like the potatoes of Shechem.

3 This urgent warning to the world is the message of the *Book of Zebediah*, the forthcoming major prophetic work from the publishers of the *Book of Obadiah* and the *Book of Habbakuk*. (Publication date: 6 June 635 BC. Price: 14.99 shekels.)

4 Controversial prophet Zebediah's raunchy study of lust and decadence in the sunbaked desert settlements of Judah and Gilead is certain to be the big headline-grabber of the season. Already a major religion is bidding for biblical rights.

5 Leading prophets who have seen the *Book of Zebediah* prior to publication predict that it could repeat the huge popular success of the *Book of Jonah*. Zebediah, says Hosea, will do for cankerworms what Jonah did for whales.

6 Often regarded by critics as a member of the so-called Minor Prophets group, Zebediah himself prefers not to be labelled. 'Woe unto the pigeonholers and them that

cry minor,' he says, 'for their inkhorns shall run dry and their retainers shall be cut off.'

7 Although he respects the great classical prophets of the past such as Isaiah and Jeremiah, he believes the whole prophecy scene has changed. 'The six and sixty chapters of Isaiah, yea, and the two and fifty chapters of Jeremiah also, are as great oaks that darken the sun,' he says thoughtfully. 'But this generation is a generation of grasshoppers. Their attention flareth like dry grass in the fire, and dieth as quickly away. Under two and fifty chapters they sink as an over-laden she-ass, and six and sixty shall be drowned by the snoring of fools.'

8 The modern prophet, he believes, has to adapt to the audience's taste. 'Let him tarry not in his task. Let him jump nimbly from the striking of thunderbolts upon the mountains of Ziph to the opening of graves in Dothan, let him haste from the depredations of locusts in Ataroth to the roaring of lions in Aphek, as the bee passeth quickly from the lily to the asphodel, nor lingereth long upon any blossom.

9 'And he that crieth Oh, how are the prophets of this generation become short of breath, how they have become minor, let him beware, for the day shall surely come when the twain do meet, and then woe unto him that hath raised his voice against us, for strong drink shall be thrown in his face, and backs most markedly turned.'

10 Zebediah will be doing a seventeen-city author tour of the Holy Land, from Dan to Beersheba, featuring readings and author signings. Beth-shemesh shall hear his words, and woe shall it be unto Beth-shemesh in that day! (12 June). Beth-horon shall be read the full horrific details of what it's like to be devoured by cankerworms, even as a dead sheep is devoured among the thorn-

bushes of Gezer, and the prophecy-lovers of Beth-horon shall be as sick as the dogs of Tishbe.

11 Zebediah will be at Prophetic Writing Week in Jezreel in July, taking part in a brains-trust with fellow-prophets Nahum and Micah on 'Whither Prophecy?'. At the Ashdod Festival in August he will give a seminar with Amos on Prophecy as a Career Option.

12 Like all prophets, Zebediah is often asked whether he prophesies regularly, or only when he feels inspired. 'The wise prophet,' he says sagely, 'sitteth down to prophesy directly he hath broken his fast, nor shall he first answer letters from them that have heard his words, nor linger to read reports of new abominations. But when the sun standeth high in the heavens, and the signs and portents visit him less readily, then is it pleasant to go to the well, and drink a stoop or two with others that labour in the same vineyard.'

13 Haggai and Malachi are among the fellow-prophets he often sees. Sometimes, he says, they talk about the semiotics of eschatology. 'But more often,' he admits laughingly, 'we raise our voices against the exactions of agents, and the faint-heartedness of publishers.'

14 In fact Zebediah has something of a reputation as a hell-raiser, which some people find surprising. 'Yet if the prophets go not among winebibbers and harlots,' he demands reasonably, 'how shall the transgressions of these be known?

15 'And he that passeth the night in this manner, when he awaketh, the light of the sun shall be heavy upon his eyelids. And there shall be a rolling of great rocks inside his head, and his mouth shall be as the dust of the wilderness. Then shall he know more fully the fruits of wickedness, and cry out more perspicaciously for repentance.'

16 He admits, like most prophets, to occasional

depression and bad patches. 'There cometh haply a morning when the prophet riseth up, and his head is as clear as the fishpools in Heshbon,' he says wryly. 'And, lo, the evil things he saw have receded away like melting snow; the harlotries of the people seem not so much harlotries as formerly; and their whoredoms understandable. Then murmureth the prophet unto himself, It may yet come to pass that the cankerworm will cease from his devourings, and the anger of the Lord will be turned aside. It may hap that we are entering upon a time of prosperity and sustained growth without concomitant inflation.'

17 In fact the horrifying consequences of this scenario for the whole future of prophetic writing are the subject of the sequel he is working on now, *2 Zebediah*, extracts from which he will be performing from September onwards as work in progress. In leading wildernesses everywhere.

Tell us everything

The phone rings. You pick it up. You're a private person, in your own home. What do you say?

You say one word. You say 'Hello.'

And you say it with an upward inflection, with the suggestion of a question mark at the end. This is dialogue of a succinctness and expressiveness that a playwright can only envy. With one short word you are simultaneously announcing your presence, offering a sample of your voice for identification, and asking your caller to identify himself in his turn.

The line can be performed in all kinds of different ways. It can suggest courtesy and patience, or irritation at being interrupted. It can convey character – a confident optimist who expects every call to be good news, a suspicious pessimist who knows it's going to be bad.

All this with one word – 'Hello?' And now here is where your performance achieves true greatness. Because whichever way you said it, at this point you stop. You sense, with the instinct of the true artist, that you have said all that needs to be said, and you say no more.

Now let's take a slightly different situation. Once again you're answering the phone. But this time it hasn't rung – not yet. You're going out, and you're recording the response that your answering machine is going to make to calls in your absence. You press the outgoing message button – and at this point all your artistry deserts you.

'Hello,' you begin, certainly – but as soon as you've said it you realise you haven't said it in the usual way.

142

There was no upward inflection, no note of query. Your voice fell instead of rising. You have no sense of an audience. You know you are talking to yourself, and you have begun to feel rather foolish. Like an actor on a bad night, you find that your whole performance is beginning to break up around you. You are not speaking politely or impatiently, confidently or cautiously. You are speaking slowly and carefully. That unresponding audience out there . . . you have a sudden uneasy feeling that it may not even understand English.

You don't trust the text any more. And so you start to try and improve upon it. 'You have reached 0467 22 983 3451,' you say, very distinctly. This is odd – you've never announced your number to me before. You don't need to. I know it. I've just dialled it. But you suspect you may not be speaking to me. You think I may be some complete stranger who has just arrived from Paraguay, ringing from a darkened phone-box with a number scribbled semi-legibly on the back of an envelope that was given him by someone he met years ago in a youth hostel in Turkey. And I may well be. But if so, why are you treating me to this great piece of oratory about *having reached* the number?

Yes, this is odder still. You are speaking not just slowly and carefully – you are speaking portentously. Never mind this non-existent visitor from Paraguay – you seem to believe you are making a statement which may be used in evidence in some future court case. You are broadcasting a last message to the world from the besieged city. You are speaking to posterity. Your words will go into the archives of recorded sound, to be cracklingly broadcast and re-broadcast in the years to come over newsreel shots of the mid-nineties.

And on you plunge. 'There is no one here to take your call right now,' you inform me solemnly. I believe I was beginning to guess as much. I think a faint suspicion was beginning to dawn upon even the man from Paraguay, who doesn't understand a word you're saying.

'But,' you say, 'if you wish to leave a message . . .'

If I *wish* to leave a message, I notice. Not if I merely *want* to. We are on a slightly higher plane of human aspiration than mere wanting. If I *wish* or *desire* to. If I *am desirous of* leaving a message. Well, why not, while we're about it? But a message for whom, I ask myself. For the nation? For all mankind?

'. . . for Warrington or Lenticula Shrubbe . . .'

Oh, for my good friends Warrington or Lenticula Shrubbe! For you two! For the very people I phoned, the ones who are not there to take my call right now! How very logical!

'. . . or for their children, Rigida and Reston . . .'

Their children? Rigida and Reston? I thought they were *your* children! What are you telling us?

'. . . or for Craxton Upstruck or Specula Gumm, who are contactable at this number until the 24th . . .'

And who I believe are that very boring couple you met on holiday last year. Yes? Why not tell us so, then? You've told us everything else. Why this sudden abandonment of full public disclosure?

But now a serious question arises. *If,* as you surmise might be the case, I wish, or desire, to leave a message for any of you, how on earth do I go about it? I put it in a bottle, perhaps? I go out and buy a carrier pigeon . . .? But what's this I hear? You're still speaking! You're telling me what to do!

'. . . then please speak clearly after the tone.'

I see. Thank you. I am to speak – not to shout, or to whistle – and to speak clearly. I am to do it after the tone. But only, of course, *if* I wish to leave a message. *If* I am moved by a volition to communicate an intelligence.

144

If I am not so moved, however, then I imagine I may speak clearly *before* the tone. I may speak *indistinctly*, either before or after it. I may mutter to myself, before, during, *and* after it . . . I may even say nothing.

In which case why don't you tell me this in so many words? Why do you leave me to work it out for myself? Why not say, quite plainly: 'If, on the other hand, you do not feel the advent of any overmastering need to communicate your thoughts to any of the aforementioned, not even to poor Specula, who never gets any messages, then you may elect to replace your receiver in silence, gently but firmly, being careful to keep it properly aligned with the base of the instrument.'

You don't because you're too busy worrying about the mess I shall make of things if I do try to leave a message.

'Kindly leave your name,' you suggest.

My name! Of course! Were desirousness of expression on my part the case then my name, indeed . . .

'And number,' you add.

And number! Yes! A shrewd suggestion! Thank you!

'It would also be helpful if you stated the time you called, and the date, together with the current weather conditions, and a note of your date of birth, next of kin, and National Insurance number.'

But before I can assemble all this information you have moved on once more. And this, I think, is going to be of particular interest to me, because now we have come to the question of what you are offering to do in return for all my efforts.

'We will call you back,' you promise, 'as soon as we can.'

You will call me back. Yes. This is the amazing proposal that your speech has been leading up to. This is what I could never have foreseen when we started out on this great journey together.

And when will you call me back? Not, as I might have guessed, when you happen to feel like it. Not when your children have grown up and left home. You will do it *as soon as you can*.

But when precisely will that be, *as soon as you can*? It will be when I am out, of course. So you won't be greeted by my usual curt 'Hello?' You will get my answering machine. You in your turn will be treated to a torrent of eloquence, a wealth of helpful suggestions about how to proceed. You will be astonished and delighted by my proposal to call *you* back.

If you're still listening at that point. Because you may have put the phone down by then, which is what a lot of my callers seem to do. So they miss all the later parts of the message, when I'm absolutely certain I'm talking to myself, in which I agonise about my terrible sense of isolation, in spite of all my efforts to communicate, and ask myself whether it's something about my manner that puts people off. Should I try to explain the workings of the answering machine more fully? Be more heartbroken about my inability to take your call?

Or should I just go *beep*, and to hell with it?

A very quiet car

Plain ordinary cowardice. That, for what it's worth, is
my uninformed personal diagnosis of what's wrong
with my car. Cowards, said Caesar, die many times before
their death, and my Audi has died seven times in the
three years I've had it.

Seven times I've gone to start it, and found it with life
entirely extinct. Seven times it has been taken in, by
Audi's excellent recovery service, to the excellent local
Audi agent, and resuscitated. They have given it two
new batteries, and changed a certain control unit, I
think, three times. They have kept it under observation
for periods of up to a fortnight. They have done everything that motor engineers can do, and done it with
genuine concern, intelligence, and determination. The
bills have all been met by Audi, even after the guarantee
expired, under the heading of 'goodwill'. Audi's goodwill
seems to be unbounded. It's mine that's becoming just a
shade strained.

I bought it because it seemed a quiet, safe, secure,
reliable, dark blue kind of car. And so indeed it has
turned out. When it's in its inactive mode it's very quiet
indeed. The diagnosticians at the garage sometimes ask
if it clicks when you turn the ignition key. The answer is
no, it doesn't even click. A click would sound like a gun
going off in the profundity of its silence. Safe? Yes – the
chances of its being involved in an accident in this mode
are as close to negligible as car-designers are ever likely
to achieve. Secure? Unstealable, I think, without a tow-

truck or a team of horses. Reliable? So far, at returning sooner or later to its peak performance in terms of quietness, safety, etc. And dark blue? Still dark blue.

It's been back in intensive care this past week, having its entire electrical system stripped out. Manuel, the recovery driver, is always remarkably good-humoured about being called out. He reminded me, laughingly, that the time before last I had for some reason become a little agitated, and had added considerably to the entertainment value of the occasion by locking the key inside the car. This time I remained very good-humoured myself. I've got used to the routine. I'm becoming institutionalised.

Also, to be fair, the car often goes. In fact it goes more often than not. But sometimes I can't help feeling that it would be nice to have a car that went a little more often still. That utter silence when you turn the key, the sudden realisation that total safety and security have descended once again, is always unnerving, even now I've achieved such serenity myself.

I worry, too, about the *car's* state of mind. I diagnose cowardice, as I said, a reluctance to go out and face the traffic. But seven total breakdowns in three years suggests some quite profound spiritual malaise. We can't just go on tinkering with the physical symptoms. We've got to get to the psychological root of the problem. One certain cure would be to drive the thing over Beachy Head. But then of course it might well not be in active mode at the crucial moment. I think the sensible alternative is to get it qualified psychiatric help.

I know exactly what's going to happen, of course. After half-an-hour on the couch in Dr Einspritz's consulting-room this silent, safe, secure, reliable, dark blue car is suddenly going to burst out in hysterical accusations. Against me, of course – who else? It's going to start

148

sobbing that I never showed it enough affection when it was new. I never washed it by hand, never shared quality time with it. Was always impatient for it to get on in life and go somewhere. The owners of all the other cars it knew bought them toys to dangle from the mirror. I never bought it so much as a yellow duster. Etcetera, etcetera.

Absolute nonsense, of course. All right, I never washed it by hand – I was a busy man – I had its insurance premiums to earn, just for a start. But I used to take it to the carwash from time to time. Buy it hot wax and wheel scrub. Not full valeting and engine clean, I accept that. I didn't think it was the sort of car that wanted to spend all day in a steam bath. I thought it was a dark blue sort of car, interested in serious personal transportation.

Well (it's going to sob), that just shows how little I ever understood it. Didn't I realise it wanted to go out and see a bit of life? To get stuck in traffic-jams occasionally with other cars, engines all going vroom-vroom together, the air thick with exhaust fumes? It was dark blue on the outside, certainly – but couldn't I see that in its heart it was fire red? I never wanted to do much but go slowly along half-empty streets, and park at parking-meters. And all the time it was longing to drive dangerously! Burn up the motorway a little! Be left at rakish angles on double yellow lines! Get towed, for heaven's sake!

Then it's going to start telling Dr Einspritz I always preferred my other machines. My word-processor, my pocket organiser. But it's not true. In my own undemonstrative way I loved that car. It's going to turn out to be jealous of the waste-disposer next! Well, at least the waste-disposer didn't sink into depressive silence. It got blocked, yes – everything gets blocked – but at least it went on struggling to cope, it went on making a kind of strangled noise.

149

Oh (the car's going to scream), what kind of love was this, that was withdrawn at the first hint of trouble? Dr Einspritz has explained that my failure as an owner has given it low self-esteem. It sees itself as a burden on the road-system, a drain on natural resources, and a threat to the environment. So every now and then it gorges on its own electricity to compensate and renders itself entirely incapable.

Dr Einspritz (it's going to go boring on) has been making a study of my articles, and has discovered that at least half of them seem to be complaints about various bits of machinery. Dr Einspritz believes that the root of the trouble is that I fear and hate machines in general.

What? – I'm going to scream. I *love* machines! I *understand* them! My relationship with machines has always been exceptionally close!

But what do the machines themselves say? With one accord (says Dr Einspritz) they switch off at the sight of me, they jam, they falter, they wipe my words and instructions out of their memories. In all their various languages they conspire to accuse me.

And of course I end up on a couch myself, being treated for abusive relationships with domestic machinery by one of Dr Einspritz's colleagues. Meanwhile Dr Einspritz contemplates my Audi, as it lies back on *his* couch, with considerable professional satisfaction. Its great outburst is over, its conflicts are resolved; it is at peace with itself at last.

Very still and quiet it lies. In fact entirely silent and motionless. Its battery's flat again.

Your shameful secret

A cold shock of apprehension ran through me when I saw Ken Follett described in the *Guardian* as a luvvie.

Ken Follett? I know *actors* are luvvies, we all know that. But Ken Follett's not an 'actor – he's a writer. So the disease is spreading. Maybe *I'm* a luvvie. I've worked with actors, shared toilet facilities with them, possibly drunk out of the wrong cup of coffee in a rehearsal room . . .

But Ken Follett doesn't even write for the theatre. And now I see that the term 'Luvvies for Labour' is being used to apply to celebrities of all descriptions. So plainly the problem is not being contained within the theatrical community at all. Everyone is at risk. Maybe *you're* a luvvie! Yes – you!

You laugh. But then you start to wonder . . . What's the first symptom?

The first symptom is that you're sitting there in a reasonably warm room, with food on the table in front of you, and a glass of wine, and you feel some faint spasm of sympathy passing through you for some other group of human beings, who as a result of their own fecklessness, or through the operation of natural laws beyond your control, are not sitting in a reasonably warm room, with food and a glass of wine in front of them.

The glass of wine in front of you is not claret, I assume – I hope. Claret-drinkers are particularly at risk – were known to be even before the luvvie virus was first identified. But you're sitting there with your glass of burgundy, say – burgundy is perfectly all right – when suddenly, out of nowhere, you hear this terrible . . . thing coming out of your mouth. This pious, sententious, canting, do-gooding, expression of hypocritical concern for someone not yourself.

How could it possibly have happened to you? You're not an actor! You haven't avoided all life's pitfalls, perhaps, but at least you've avoided that one. It's true you thought of taking it up when you were at school. And you could have done – everyone said you were a wonderful Bernardo in the school *Hamlet*. By now, if you hadn't exercised real self-discipline, you could easily have been sitting in the Groucho giving interviews about European monetary policy. But you steeled yourself. You turned your back on it. You didn't become a writer, either, though God knows you were tempted at times. You didn't even go into cultural administration or arts funding. Remember how you almost responded to that advertisement in the Careers pages? Forgotten yearnings come flooding back. . . . But you didn't. And now, suddenly, out of nowhere . . . *this*.

Another terrible suspicion comes to you. Perhaps you are a member of *the chattering classes*! You cast your mind back. What have you been saying at dinner parties recently? Nothing, surely. You sat there, you ate your food, you drank your . . . well, it might have been claret – but claret on its own is all right. It's claret and concern for others which is such a deadly cocktail. And you certainly didn't express any concern for others, not in public, not at the dinner table. You smiled a little sardonically when other people spoke. And all right, you spoke, of course you spoke, you're only human – but you always practised safe speech. You talked about the kind of things that the non-chattering classes talk about. Schools, holidays. How you don't understand computers. The ridicu-

152

lousness of luvvies and members of the chattering classes. But chatter? No one could call that chatter . . .

And then you remember . . . it was late at night, you'd had quite a lot of the claret, and you dropped your guard a little. You were just fooling around, of course, it wasn't serious. It was something that the person sitting opposite you said. Something about luvvies or the chattering classes, perhaps. For some reason you felt you wanted to disagree. Some actors, you said, were perfectly decent people who knew their place. And if the chattering classes didn't chatter, then what would the non-chattering classes have to non-chatter about?

Maybe, you think, nobody else remembers – maybe they never even noticed. But *you* know it happened. *You* know that deep down you have these strange unacknowledged feelings. *You* know you were tipping claret down on top of them. And next time you go to a dinner-party you're going to be looking at everyone, thinking 'Does *he* know about me? Does *she* know?' And just as you think you're getting away with it once again you'll realise that there's something familiar about the person who's looking at you across the table, not saying anything, a little ironical smile playing about the lips . . . Yes – it's someone who was present the night you committed your little indiscretion.

You try to keep calm, but you feel the panic rising within you. He *knows* – you know that from the little smile. Is he going to out you to the rest of the company? Is he going to ring you at work next day, as you sit among all your carefully-chosen, discreet, unforthcoming, intensely non-theatrical colleagues, and try to blackmail you?

Or worse, suggest meeting somewhere privately, just the two of you? Because you realise, from that little smile, that he is a secret luvvie himself, a closet member

153

of the chattering classes. He'll take you to some special bar he knows, full of actors and people in leather jackets flaunting progressive opinions. He'll ply you with claret. You'll find yourself exchanging shy doubts about the enterprise culture and the sovereignty of Parliament ...

As you sit there at the dinner-table, the whole vertiginous downward spiral opens in front of you. You make a supreme effort to avoid your fate. You start to babble wildly about schools and holidays – the incomprehensibility of computers and Stephen Hawking – the difficulty of finding good servants – the prospects for the stag-hunting season ...

Everyone gazes at you. They've never seen you like this before – so red in the face, so fearless of received opinion and political correctness, so profoundly unchattering. The man opposite goes on smiling his little smile, but now it simply drives you to bolder and bolder achievements. You denounce Europe – and Asia for good measure. You call for the return of the death penalty for trespassing and being foreign.

You begin to feel wildly exhilarated. You realise you're doing something you've never done before ... Until suddenly it dawns on you what it is.

You're acting.

Outside story

... So, provided the scheme to build low-cost weekend housing on the estate is accepted by the local planning authority, it looks as if the cherry orchard itself has been saved from the axe. More on that later. Now back to the main story of the evening. Are you there, Michael?

Yes, Trevor, I am.

How are things outside the National Theatre?

Well, it's a fine night out here, Trevor, with a bit of a breeze off the river. But inside it's pretty tense. The good news is that they're still in there, and they're still talking. Some of the talking, by all accounts, has been pretty tough – Hamlet himself, I gather, has not pulled his punches. It's been a long evening – this is the feeling here – and it's going to go on for quite a bit longer yet.

Any developments in the situation since we last talked to you?

Trevor, it's too early to tell. But I was talking to someone who was inside the theatre in the last half-hour or so, and he said there were plans at court for a bit of a family get-together, which must I think be a good sign.

A get-together?

I understand it involves some sort of home theatricals.

No fears that the King might be tempted to take a tougher line?

Oh, I don't think so, Trevor.

There were some pretty wild allegations flying about earlier.

Yes, but there is a great determination here not to let the peace process be derailed, and most of the people I've spoken to remain pretty hopeful about the outcome.

There's no sense of déjà-vu *about all this?*

Yes, Trevor, some old hands have been saying 'We've seen all this before, and if we don't learn from past mistakes we could just end up with a real disaster on our hands.'

So the next hour or two could be crucial?

They could, Trevor, but the King has already brought two younger men on to his team who are known to be close to Hamlet, in a very clear gesture of conciliation. It may or may not be significant that the Prince is to make an official visit to England, which should help to take the steam out of the situation a little.

Is the Prince showing any signs of strain?

He has been showing some signs of the enormous pressure he is under, yes. He's made a number of major speeches in the last hour or two, but quite what effect they've had on opinion here it's too early to tell.

Is that the Prince we can see now, just behind you?

No, that's one of the local dossers being thrown out of the theatre by security men. If you'd been here earlier you'd have seen quite a lot of coming and going just behind me there. Quite a lot of stiff drinks being drunk. Quite a lot of visits to the toilets. But things have quietened down in the last few minutes.

156

So you feel the signs are good?

I'm pretty hopeful, Trevor, provided they can just keep talking. They've been talking now for the best part of two hours, and the longer they go on the more likely it is we're going to see them shake hands and issue a joint communiqué.

But if the talks do break down . . . ?

Then it's anybody's guess. The consequences are incalculable. We could, I think, see a distinct worsening of relations. We might even end up with the King and the Prince not on speaking terms.

No chance that it could even end in violence?

Well, we hope it won't come to that! It's in everybody's interest to keep calm and behave sensibly. They'll probably keep us all on tenterhooks until the last possible moment, but the smart money here is on wedding bells before too long.

Michael Brunson, thank you. Now, the rest of the news. Fire broke out this evening in Valhalla, home of many of the world's best-known gods. Local fire chiefs say that the blaze is now under control. And in Spain a wealthy playboy has had the novel idea of inviting a statue to dinner! The statue duly turned up, and by all accounts thoroughly enjoyed its evening out. That's it for now! Have a good weekend.

Service with a smile

'As you are aware,' begins a letter that arrived the other day, '*x* Computer Services is your encumbrant service provider.'

Well, no, in point of fact, I was *not* aware that *x* Computer Services was (or even were) my encumbrant service provider. I thought they were the people I had a maintenance contract with to repair various pieces of electronic apparatus when they go wrong. It comes as a slight surprise to discover that I have such a thing as an encumbrant service provider.

A pleasant surprise, certainly. I shall drop it into the conversation when you are going on rather tiresomely about the wonderful little man you have who adjusts your bannisters, or tunes your euphonium. 'If you ever need any encumbrant service,' I shall say, 'you might do worse than try the provider I have.' You'll be shaken. You haven't got an encumbrant service provider yourself. The need for encumbrant service has never arisen in your rather less sophisticated lifestyle. You're not absolutely certain, if you're honest, what encumbrant service is.

So you probably wouldn't understand the rest of the letter, either. It's all written in a very elevated style, which I think may be a little above your head, but which evokes confidence and respect in those of us who know how to appreciate the finer things of life.

'We understand,' it says, 'in times like these IT Departments are under extreme pressure to provide internal services to there users. We are uniquely positioned to assist your organisation with a full portfolio of additional value added services . . . As you are already a valued customer of *x*, we can . . . encompass additional services within your existing contract.' And they offer me a choice of On-site Resource and Outsourcing.

You gape. You didn't know I was an IT Department, as well as a man of letters and connoisseur of fine wines. You never realised what pressure I was under to provide internal service to various there users. The concept of a there user is probably beyond you for a start. Look, there are here users like me, yes? Here I am, using here in various ways – sitting, talking, etc. – no mystery about it. You understand that? Well, then there are also users who are not here but there. There they are, using there. But to do this they require internal services from here.

Which we poor IT Departments have to provide! Oh, yes, we earn our outsourcing all right, especially in times like these – because I don't have to tell you what times like these are like. So I'm particularly glad to be offered not only additional services but *value-added* ones. And to be offered them not in a plastic carrier-bag, but in a *portfolio*, ready to be *encompassed*. And not by some scruffy street-trader propped up against a lamp-post, but by someone *uniquely positioned*.

It's embarrassing to watch you struggle with all this. All right, let me go back to the beginning and explain to you what *encumbrant service* is. It's service so elaborate and gracious as to be a positive encumbrance to the less socially adept. You remember when you were staying in a grand hotel somewhere, and you picked up the phone to order a boiled egg from room-service? And you knew you'd get such a flourishing of napery and single-stem-med roses, such a flashing of smiles and a whipping-off of covers, and that you'd be required to perform such a nervous jumping up and down and smiling and thanking in return, such a juggling with gratuities which may or may not have been included in the bill, that you put the phone down again?

Well, that's encumbrant service, and a man of the world like myself is perfectly at home with it. One of the machines that x Computer Services look after is on the blink now, as it happens. If it were yours you'd pick the phone up, then realise you couldn't just blurt out in ordinary uncultivated English to service providers as grand as these that the screen was all kind of jiggering about, and you'd give up and go out for a hamburger once again.

Whereas I put on my special voice for talking to earls and above, and I say easily ... Well, let me just practise in front of the mirror for a moment.

'I do most tremendously regret being encumbrant upon you, but I seem to be positioned so that I am requirant ... requisant ... of on-site resourcing ... outsourcing ... out-site onsourcing. Could you encompass this? I should explain that I am a servicee of yours. A receivee of your valued service ... your value-added service ... your valuable additional service with added value. I am, I should perhaps explain, a here user. A here and now user. A here and in-times-like-these user.

'Or rather was, until my equipment became service-requisant. I am a here and formerly in-times-like-these user. An existing here and formerly in-this-day-and-age user. An ex-existing user who is urgently desirous of becoming a re-existing user.

'The thing is, the screen's on the blink ... Sorry! – I mean on the nictitate ... It's gone all kind of funny ... has become in some sense inducive of cacchination ... inductive of risibility ... Well, let's not beat about the bush, let's not flagellate about the berberis. It's afflicted by an encumbrancy ... positioned in discommodant

160

mode . . . internally subfunctional . . . functionally value-deficient . . . defective in its functional modality . . .

'Anyway, I am desirous of achieving disencumbrancy of this encumbrancy. Would you be positioned to offer, ex-portfolio, external service to which value had been added, where the value in question resides in the successful encompassment of the value-added service?

'And if so, could you do it in times like these? I mean, in times *remarkably* like these? In times more like these than tomorrow will be?

'May I say how much value I should esteem to be added to your already valued offer if you could extend its presently existing potentiality into fully potentialised existence?'

You see? That's what I call *style*. It needs a little effort, but it's so encumbering.

A good stopping place

How on earth did I get into this situation?

I mean, at the start of another piece, which is appearing exactly a week after the last piece, which was exactly a week after the piece before it . . . How has this come about? I wrote a regular column when I was a young man for a number of years. Then I stopped. I stopped because I didn't want to grow old and find I was still at the start of another piece, which was appearing exactly a week after, etc. Now I've grown old and what do I find? I find I'm still at the start of another piece, which is appearing, etc.

Let me try and work out what happened. I had a little time in hand last year when I couldn't start any major new project, because I was waiting for directors for plays, and so on. So I wrote a short piece or two, to keep by me for a rainy day. What sort of rainy day? I don't know. Sometimes a piece is required. It's not a bad idea to have one in the store-cupboard, along with the two tins of sardines and the packet of dry biscuits that was best before April 1987.

Then I remembered a few more ideas I'd put by over the years, and I wrote a few more pieces. I think there were about eight of them. Eight seemed a good round number, not too few and not too many. I sent them off to the *Guardian*. I had not the faintest intention that this should be the start of any regular arrangement. This was a limited engagement, as they say in the theatre.

Eight weeks only. Season must end on such-and-such a date due to prior commitments.

The articles started to appear. 'How do you like writing a column again?' people asked me, in the carefully pleasant tone of voice one might adopt if one was remarking to an alcoholic that he seemed to be holding a drink in his hand, in case he hadn't noticed himself. It wasn't a column, I explained. It was a series of articles, a limited engagement. They smiled. I was just going to have the odd drink and then stop again, was I? They'd heard that kind of story before.

And indeed, as the end of this limited season approached, to stop at that particular point began to seem a bit . . . *odd* . . . Eight didn't seem to be such a good number, now I'd got to it. Wouldn't it be more natural to stop after nine, or ten? Ten, yes. Ten was a good, natural, self-explanatory number. I could say to people – I could say to *myself*, Well, I'm just writing ten pieces . . . No, I couldn't. You can't just casually happen to do ten of something. What you *can* do – nonchalantly, who's counting? – is *a dozen*.

All right, so a dozen. But then to write exactly twelve pieces seems a penny-pinching, mean-spirited way of justifying talk of a dozen. Make it a baker's dozen. No, make it fourteen. Then I can talk about a dozen and have the private satisfaction of knowing that I'm generously understating it.

So, I'll stop after fourteen. But then fourteen . . . that's just about enough for people to have noticed they were under way. So they'll notice if there isn't a fifteenth. They'll think I've been fired. Caught stealing the petty cash. Drunk in charge of the fax machine.

Better hang on for a few more. Slip away after twenty, say. No surprise if I went after twenty. Everyone's on short contracts these days. No one's hanging around

163

waiting for the pension and the chiming clock. Nothing has a permanent structure any more. Be a bit of a surprise if I stuck around *after* twenty, in fact. People might start thinking I'd got into a groove, couldn't think of anything else to do, was suffering from some form of neurotic compulsion.

Which *I* know is nonsense, of course. All the same, once you've got up into the twenties it is starting to look more and more like a regular column. The enterprise is acquiring a certain momentum of its own, a certain historical gravitas. Its beginnings are getting lost in the mists of time. There are several million people in the world who hadn't even been born when this thing started. It would have been all right if I'd stopped after eight, I see that now. Eight's nothing. But twenty . . . twenty-five – it's starting to be part of the great chain of being, a short but significant fibre in the ongoing texture of the universe. It's becoming an institution. It's like a chain letter, or the monarchy. Totally pointless, but to break the chain now seems somehow wilful, violent, unthinkable.

Isn't this how things start? Alcoholism, relationships – or indeed the monarchy. You have a few drinks with your friends when you're a young man. You go out with someone a couple of times. You crown two or three insignificant local kings. Then you find yourself in the pub fairly regularly . . . She comes round to your place, you go round to hers . . . The kings beget a few more kings . . .

And before you know what's happened the habit has taken over. One moment you're enjoying the odd Ethelred, one or two Edwys, everything very civilised and delightful – stop any time, no problem – you might put in a nice warlord as dictator instead, if you feel like it, or elect some Professor of Theology as president – and

164

the next thing you know you've had eight Edwards, eight Henrys, four Georges, four Williams, not to mention two Elizabeths and a few odd Victorias and Matildas – in fact you've lost count – you're right out of control – and you *can't* stop now, not just before your third Charles . . .!

I don't want to be that sort of person. I want to be the sort of person who can take it or leave it. Come and go. Put things down, pick them up. Work one day, have fun the next. Enjoy a king or two, then switch perfectly happily to a General Secretary. Chuck the chain-letter in the waste-paper basket, let the funnel-web spider die out, avoid the cracks in seven paving stones and then cheerfully step on the eighth . . . ninth . . . tenth . . . no, no . . . twelfth . . . fourteenth . . . sixteenth . . . no, no, no! Nineteenth . . . twenty-first . . . stop!

So I'm striking a blow for sanity and freedom. *Tout passe, tout casse, tout lasse*. Before you're *lassé* and I'm *cassé*, I *passe*. I'm stopping. Not after a hundred, or a hundred and forty-four. Not in the year 2,000, or on my ninetieth birthday, or to celebrate the coronation of Queen Diana. After the however-manyeth, on the wherever-we've-got-to-th of whichever month it happens to be.

I've got a bottle of very expensive vintage champagne that a friend gave me about twelve years ago. I've still got it because I couldn't think of an occasion sufficiently definitive to justify ending its venerable existence, and it looked set to continue undrunk forever. But I'm going to open it today, without any occasion for it at all, except to celebrate a small victory of spontaneity over habit, of reason over obsession, of stopping right here, bang in the middle of

First service

Tonight they are holding my favourite service, the Annual Service for People in Advertising, in All Souls, Langham Place – and the sixth in the series, no less.

Still, not everyone in the advertising industry will find the somewhat traditional atmosphere of All Souls congenial. Since the moral welfare of advertising men is a subject close to my heart, may I recommend the Harvest Festival which CADCAR (the Congress of Advertising, Confidence, and Allied Racketeers) is holding in St Swiz's, and which many in the industry will find more up-to-date and relevant in its approach? For those who are thinking of going, here is the order of service:

HYMN
We put our trust in Swiz,
For only Swiz has Fiz, etc.

LESSON
From the Book of Amazing Free Offers
1. These are the generations of Swiz. Thomas Noggin begat Joseph Noggin; and Thomas Noggin and Son begat Noggin *Holdings*; and Noggin Holdings begat Noggin (England) Ltd; *and* Noggin (England) Ltd begat Oho.
2. And Oho begat Fub; and Fub begat Guf; and Guf begat Swiz; and Swiz begat twelve million pounds.

RESPONSES

Blessed be the name of Swiz.
> *Let the name of Swiz be praised.*
The hoardings shall blazon it forth.
> *And the air shall be loud with the clamour of it.*
On the page it shall be written.
> *On the page, yea, across two pages.*
In special supplements shall it be sounded forth.
> *And bruited even in the editorials.*

(The copywriters and public relations men walk in procession to the front, bearing pieces of copy, designs for cereal packets, plastic giveaways, samples of tournedos and whisky they have bought for journalists, and newspaper cuttings of stories they have originated. These offerings are judged by a panel of well-known television personalities, and Golden Calf statuettes are awarded as prizes.)

(Here endeth the first part)

> *It's new! It's true! It's made for you!*
> *For knees in trousers, knees in cassocks,*
> *You cannot better CADCAR HASSOCKS!*
> *CADCAR! CADCAR! CADCAR!*

(Here beginneth part two)

LESSON
From the Second Book of Unsolicited Testimonials

1. There dwelt in the *town* of Screwe, that is over against Twicester, a certain poor woman.
2. And it came to pass that unto her appeared a man in *shining raiment* that said: I am come from Swiz, and am sent forth by him to inquire if there be any in this city that *keep* his name in honour.

167

3. For unto him that keepeth his name in honour shall be given cause for rejoicing, and great increase shall be his.

4. Then saith the poor woman: all my life I have kept faith with Swiz, and *have not deserted* him. And lo, she shewed the man her Swiz, which was of *family size*. And he drew forth from his scrip two more Swiz, and gave them to the woman, saying: Thou faithful servant, thy treasure is multiplied threefold.

5. And he saith unto her: Unto those that keep faith with Swiz, with them shall Swiz also keep faith. For that which is white shall be whitest; and that which is whitest shall be whiter than white. Ten thousand are the women that have witnessed unto this miracle, and it is written: Can ten thousand women be wrong?

6. And the woman was amazed, and gave thanks, and magnified the name of Swiz.

SERMON

On the text from the Book of Fub: 'Shall a man labour for truth, when that which is not true comforteth multitudes? For truth is like the butter that was put unto the test. An hundred women partook thereof, and of those hundred were there nine and ninety that were deceived, and knew not the false butter from the true. For the false butter was smooth and finely apparelled, and they knew it not.'

HYMN

Who would an adman be
Hymning sweet fictions,
Must labour valiantly
'Gainst state restrictions.

Consumers flee away,
I'll fear not what they say,
I'll call the night the day,
To be an adman.

Second service

I'm sorry to say that the helping hand I tried to offer my
friends in the advertising industry in the last piece by
announcing (free of charge) the order of service for the
advertising men's Harvest Festival at St Swiz's was not too
well received.

The hardest things of all were said by Mr Mark
Chapman-Walker, a director of Television Wales and West,
about the extract from the article which later appeared on
BBC Television. It was, he said, 'so staggering in its
irreverence, bad taste, and general unfunniness that I am
not surprised that a large number of people complained'.

Mr Chapman-Walker is also a director of the *News of the
World*, so his views on matters of taste command respect.
In fact I have decided that the best thing I can do is to go
right back to the beginning, and give the details of the
service in St Swiz's with an attempt at the reverence, good
taste, and general funniness which in the good old days
made Mr Chapman-Walker's paper the trusted and res-
pected companion of eight million families every sabbath.

THE VICAR AND THE WOMAN IN THE FRONT PEW

What a vicar alleged he saw going on quite openly in his
own church at Harvest Festival was described yesterday
when Michael Frayn, a journalist, of 29 Tregunter Road,
Screwe, was found guilty on three charges of irreverent
staggeringness, gustatory badness, and general humour-
lessness.

The Reverend Harold Admore, vicar of St Swiz's, said that he had held a Harvest Festival for advertising men. But his first reaction to what met his eyes on entering the church was one of disgust. In answer to a question, he replied it was the smallness of the congregation that had disgusted him.

SEX MIX-UP

Admore said that besides the men there were a number of women present. The sexes were mixed. He thought that some of the women had been brought by the men, but that others had 'simply walked in on their own from the street'. Many of the women were wearing make-up and high heels.

ASSOCIATED WITH COLOURED MAN

Admore stated that he took as the subject of his sermon man's quest for good, likening it to the skilled tracking which was associated with the Red Indian. His intentions throughout the alleged incidents, he said, had been entirely honourable.

Miss E. Grewsom said that she had been sitting in the front pew all the time that the events mentioned were alleged to have been taking place. She agreed that the vicar had used certain words. They were clearly audible from where she was sitting. She also saw him make certain gestures.

SHOCKED

She recalled distinctly that at the end of the first hymn, and on several other occasions, the vicar had used a four-lettered word. It had stuck in her mind, she said, because of the tone of voice in which he had uttered it, and because it seemed to be constantly on the lips of everyone present, women as well as men.

170

Under cross-examination, Miss Grewsom admitted that she had been shell-shocked while serving with the ATS.

NOT HIS BABY

Mr P. J. Nunbetter, a church-warden, gave evidence that he had heard Admore make a certain suggestion to a younger man. As a result of this suggestion, the younger man had played the first hymn.

Nunbetter said he did not remember which hymn it was, since the musical side was 'not his baby'.

INDULGED IN ORGY

Questioned about money that was alleged to have changed hands during the evening, Mr R. O. Platter, another church-warden, admitted that he had collected it.

He said he did not know how much was involved, and that it was none of his business to ask what services were expected in return for the money.

'My job is simply to collect it,' he said. 'You seem to think I had nothing better to do than to indulge in an orgy of speculation.'

NOTHING ON

In a statement, Admore was alleged to have admitted being a miserable sinner, but to have added: 'The police have nothing on me.' His wife gave evidence that he had always behaved perfectly normally, so far as she knew.

As stated, Frayn was found guilty on all three charges, and sentenced to five years' corrective reading of the *News of the World*.

Whereas

(A) The Author of this Deed is at present seised in fee simple and in stupor tremens by the process of moving house.

(B) The Author is of sound mind SAVE THAT the Vendor of the first part and the Mortgagee of the second part and the Assignor of the third part and the Leaseholder of the fourth part and the Lessee of the fifth part and the Curtainor of the sixth part and the Carpetee of the seventh part and the Gasholder of the eighth part HAVE AGREED to cover all floors walls tables and other surfaces in the present residence of the Author with three coats of prime quality LEGAL DOCUMENTS.

(C) The aforementioned legal documents are close carpeted throughout with verbiage of a tasteful period character.

Provided that

A space shall be kept clear among the said verbiage to accommodate an Excise Stamp charged at NOT MORE than one third of the Government's current defence expenditure.

And wherethemore

(A) For a consideration the Solicitors of the aforementioned parties have agreed to join in these deeds SEEING THAT no aforementioned party would really go with a swing without them.

172

(B) Given the slightest additional consideration the Solicitors' Solicitors and the Solicitors' Solicitors' Solicitors would doubtless also join in both in fee simple and fee compound.

Provided that

The aforementioned partygiver (hereinafter called 'the Mortgaged Soul') shall not be responsible for maintaining more than half the country's legal profession at any one time.

And wherewithstanding

IN THE EVENT of a person being both Vendor of one property and Vendee of another it is required by Logic that the Market cannot be unfavourable to him in both capacities.

EXCEPT THAT in the case of the Author the Market shall be guaranteed to be permanently against him whether as Vendor Vendee or Vendsoever.

And whereasmuchas

(A) The Friends of the Author (hereinafter called Christopher and Lavinia Crumble) bought purchased or became seised of their demesne two years ago for the sum of ONE THOUSAND POUNDS (£1,000).

(B) The value of the said demesne THEREUPON without let or hindrance and without prejudice to the liberal reputation of the aforesaid Christopher and Lavinia Crumble rose to TEN THOUSAND POUNDS (£10,000).

(C) This being achieved in part by the application of two coats of pale mauve paint by the said Christopher Crumble and in part by the removal of all adjacent tenants of immoral or drunken habits or small means and their replacement by new tenants of immoral or drunken habits and more substantial means.

And wheremoresoever

Even those Friends of the Author known as Horace and Doris Morris ordinarily situate in the same boat as the Author and generally supposed by the Author to be at least as fee simple about these matters as himself have acquired a residence the size of a small cathedral for A SONG (1 Sng).

And wherewithas

(A) In contradistinction to the Morrises and Crumbles the Author of this Deed (or Doer or Deedee) shall entertain all reasonable certainty that he will hereinafter be known as the Deedled or Done.

(B) The Author shall hereupon feel himself personally responsible for the maintenance in good condition of the Property Market heretofore known as the Property Racket.

(C) The Author shall be absolutely entitled to feel ground floor flat by the whole business.

Now it is agreed

The Author shall have in perpetuity the peaceful enjoyment of the dirty end of the stick.

Now this deed

WITNESSETH as follows:

The Author solemnly covenants with himself that notwithstanding overcrowding dilapidation infestation sudden enrichment sudden impoverishment conjugal representations or the purchase by Horace and Doris Morris of a royal palace in good order for fifteen shillings and sixpence NOR EVEN WITHSTANDING unemployment need and hunger among the Legal Profession HE SHALL before he contemplates moving house again meditate deeply upon this document for three calendar months following the first full moon after the penultimate Quarter Day of the next Leap Year but one.

In witness whereof the party hereto sets hereunder his exhausted hand.

Composition for ten hands

The admiration and respect which I feel for Kingsley Amis, John Braine, Robert Conquest, Edmund Crispin, Iain Hamilton, Anthony Hartley, Bernard Levin, Simon Raven, David Rees and Peregrine Worsthorne severally is as nothing to the awe in which I hold their corporate talent. They know whose side they are on in Vietnam, and have written in a body to *The Times* twice now to announce their verdict to the world.

I wish I knew which side I was on. But I don't; and the more I read about Vietnam, the less able I am to pick a team. No such indecision hinders Amis, Braine, Conquest, Crispin, Hamilton, Hartley, Levin, Raven, Rees and Worsthorne. 'When all the lesser issues are cleared away,' they asked themselves, 'whose side are we on?' And at once they replied: 'Our answer must be that we unequivocally support America and her allies . . .'

There was heartfelt relief in Washington, naturally, when the State Department found they had the unequivocal support of ten English men of letters. Weary troops in Vietnam took heart to learn that Amis, Braine, Conquest and Crispin were right there, but a short 7,000 miles behind them, not to mention Hamilton, Hartley and Levin, or Raven, Rees and Worsthorne.

But then another letter appeared in *The Times*, penned by Brigid Brophy, Peter Buckman, Anthony Burgess, Ivy Compton-Burnett, Len Deighton, Gillian Freeman, B. S. Johnson, Julian Mitchell, John Mortimer, Alan Sillitoe and William Trevor, deploring the idea of unequivocal support for American policy in Vietnam.

'... Considering the available information on this atrocious war,' argued Brophy, Buckman, Burgess, Compton-Burnett, Deighton, Freeman, Johnson, Mitchell, Mortimer, Sillitoe and Trevor, 'we do not believe that the policies of America and her allies are likely to bring about the peace which is earnestly desired by all.'

The mood of elation in Washington slumped when this copy of *The Times* arrived. As the State Department's statistical experts can scarcely have failed to notice, they have ten writers for them, and eleven against. And I have the impression that the writers who are opposed to American policy have on average written more books than the writers who are in favour of it. Which must count for something in Washington and Hanoi. Mustn't it?

But there are other teams of writers who have yet to speak – as I discovered at a little literary soirée the other night when I was introduced to K. D. Haddock, Walter Pinn, Pennington Pownall, O. J. Sprout, and Thorsten Trouncer.

'What?' I cried. ' Not *the* K. D. Haddock, Walter Pinn, Pennington Pownall, O. J. Sprout and Thorsten Trouncer? The authors of that marvellous little letter on decimal coinage, and that very stylish missive against racial provocation in Fiji?'

They blushed.

'The same,' they murmured.

Well, I told them what a terrific admirer I was of their stuff – what a deeply personal style and individual view of the world I thought they had.

'Whenever I come up against some rather tricky subject,' I told them, 'such as the wage-structure of the Bolivian tin industry, I always think to myself: "I wonder what Haddock, Pinn, Pownall, Sprout and Trouncer would say about that."'

They were very bucked.

'We think we speak for all of us,' they said, 'when we say

that we're as pleased as a dog with two tails. If not five dogs with ten tails.'

I asked them if they were working on another letter.

'No,' they said. 'At the moment we're working on a critical edition of the love-letters of Drossel, Gudney, Lidless and Nane, to Adbrow, Bantling, Cold-Brightman and Zimmer. It's one of the great literary romances – in the end they married, and had twenty-three children.'

Anyway, when they found out that I was Frayn, of Barnold, Brevis, Frayn, Frowder and Straithwaite, they were kind enough to say that they rather admired some of our work, too – particularly our Middlesex dialect stories, and our relentless opposition to the entry of Ireland into the Common Market.

After a bit, of course, we got round to the problems facing writers today.

'You can't get over it,' sighed Haddock, Pinn, Pownall, Sprout and Trouncer, 'the days of the old one-man-band type of writer are pretty well over.'

Barnold, Brevis, Frowder, Straithwaite and I agreed.

'We mean,' said Haddock, Pinn, Pownall, Sprout, and Trouncer, 'we'd never have been able to make up our minds about decimal coinage in the way we did if there hadn't been five of us.'

'What we personally feel,' said Barnold, Brevis, Frowder, Straithwaite and I, 'is that if there were ten or eleven of us, as in the Amis outfit, or the Brophy concern, we might be able to stand back far enough from the details to come down clearly and unambiguously on one side or the other in Vietnam.'

Because the truth is, of course, that today writers have got to merge and amalgamate to survive, just like everybody else. Big issues demand big thoughts; and big thoughts require big teams of thinkers.

Anyway, we're all going to write to *The Times* about it.

Almost too utterly common entrance

'A most unusual seminar,' says the heading on an advertisement which has been appearing in undergraduate magazines recently. The advertisement is issued by a firm who describe themselves as 'the most brilliant of all the advertising agencies,' looking for 'the most brilliant of all this year's graduands.'

'They propose to invite up to twenty of you,' it continues, 'after a long interrogation in London, to spend a weekend with them during the Easter vacation. The hospitality at this weekend will be almost vulgarly profuse. Continual distraction will be offered. But there will also be one written paper of the most taxing kind. It will need great stamina to endure it all.'

It certainly will if this is anything like the weekend which Harris-Harris, the brighter than brightest agency, hold each year at Wosby Hall, the ancestral home of the Selection-Board family. Here the daiquiris flow like water, served by top models in fishnet stockings, while fashionable dance bands play softly among the Picassos.

'The ambience here,' says Garth Peacock, one of the agency men assigned to the job, waving an odoriferous Balkan cigarette at the time-hallowed setting, ' is almost, *comment dit-on*, vulgarly profuse, don't you think?'

'Er, yes,' mumbles R. Slodge, former President of the Oxford Union. Garth Peacock presses a tiny pocket transmitter key which registers at headquarters the damning comment *'This man considers himself superior to popular cultural values.'*

179

'Have another cigar, Nubbs,' says Peacock to the former Cambridge stroke. 'Er, no thanks,' replies Nubbs, and Peacock signals ruthlessly *'Deficient in phallic motivation'.* Nubbs passes the solid gold humidor on to Cropper, once editor of the *Isis,* but Cropper, who has smoked five cigars already, shakes his head queasily. Peacock adds another comment to the Nubbs report: *'Complete failure to persuade in face of difficult market conditions'.*

'I hope,' says Peacock, 'you're not all finding the weekend too utterly boring?'

'Not me,' replies Potkin, the noted Oxford actor, gesturing for another bottle of champagne. 'Can't soak the stuff up fast enough.' (*'A certain lack of moral fibre',* signals Peacock.)

'Oh, far from it,' adds Mark Smoothe, undergraduate son of the Minister of Chance and Speculation, also ordering another bottle. ' I think the amenities we are enjoying here are a fitting background to the sort of seminar which, today more than ever, plays an absolutely vital part in the progressive development of the free world.' (*'A brilliant creative mind',* transmits Peacock.)

'Where's the lavatory?' demands Cropper urgently. (*'A poor ability to choose language that brings out the most attractive aspects of a subject',* notes Peacock.)

By the time Cropper has hacked his way back through the almost vulgarly deep pile of the carpet, bowing footmen have ushered the whole party on to the luxuriously appointed assault course, where Roscoe is waiting to put them through an almost disgustingly elegant initiative test.

'What we should like you to do,' he explains, 'if it's not too almost utterly tedious, is to imagine that this ditch is full of synthetic raspberry jam. You have to get the synthetic raspberry jam over this wall of consumer resistance without touching the real raspberry jam made by the same

180

firm. To do it you've got nothing but four feet of tarred twine, two empty oil drums, one model in black lace underwear, and £100,000 . . .'

When the fleet of Rolls-Royces takes them back to the almost sickeningly exquisite house, they face the most testing moment of all. One by one they are shown into the presence of J. B., the head of the agency himself, as he sits in the Sheraton Room surrounded by Cellini champagne-coolers and Fabergé foot-warmers.

'Sit down, Mr Nubbs,' he murmurs in an almost insupportably aristocratic tone. 'Tell me, Mr Nubbs, do you believe in God?'

'Er, well, I, er . . .'

'Of course you do. Take a cigar and then sell me the idea in fifty punchy, easy-to-read words.'

Yes, it certainly demands stamina. And remember, stamina demands Fub, for only new wonder Fub has magic Zub!

Scrapbook for 1964

It was a wonderful summer that year. Everyone seemed to be at the seaside, enjoying the long sunlit days without a care in the world ...

It was the year of the Mods and Rockers ... of 'Can't Buy Me Love' and 'Anyone Who Had a Heart'. Everyone was dancing the Shake, the Block and the Blue Beat. In America a man brought out a two-piece swimsuit with only one piece ...

But over it all hung a shadow. For this was 1964 – the twenty-fifth anniversary of the outbreak of the Second World War. In grim sunless offices all over Europe hard-faced men in shirtsleeves were plotting to unleash upon the world the most terrible campaign of war memoirs, war films, war poetry, war photographs, war histories and war reappraisals that mankind had ever seen ...

Among the crowds in Britain as the crisis drew on that fateful summer was one man who sunbathed and danced the Shake with a somewhat pensive expression. From time to time he would stop singing 'Anyone Who Had a Heart' for a moment, and thoughtfully jot down something on a scrap of paper. A perfectly ordinary man, you might have said, jotting something down on a perfectly ordinary scrap of paper ...

But what he was writing was a diary – a minute-by-minute account of his experiences in that fateful year. His intention was to place it in a sealed envelope for publication on the twenty-fifth anniversary of the outbreak of the Great Memoir War, as a form of endowment assurance for his old age. We are privileged to be able to publish it now, twenty-five years ahead of its time.

Thursday: Lunch at Reggie Tooth's with the Dicky Dymchurches and Sandy Troon. The talk is of nothing but the crisis – the papers are full of it every day. Only the *Daily Express* strikes a more hopeful note – 'No War Anniversary This Year'. They argue that only a hopeless pessimist could believe that the silver anniversary of the Second World War would fall in the same year as the golden anniversary of the First. They say the conjunction must be the result of some official muddle.

I ask Reggie, who has highly placed contacts in the diary and calendar industry, if he thinks there might be anything in this. He says he thinks not, and I'm afraid he is right. We have managed to turn a blind eye to the ominous events of the last few years – we did nothing about the anniversary of Caesar's invasion of Britain in 1945; we looked the other way in 1955, when we were faced with the 500th anniversary of the outbreak of the Wars of the Roses. But I've met no one who doesn't think we're in for it this time.

Friday: Sunshine, ripe corn, red apples warm to the touch – the grim old portents of impending war memoirs are everywhere. I cannot help recalling with a shudder the blazing summer of 1959, when we numbly watched the remorseless approach of the 105th anniversary of the Crimean War.

Spend the afternoon looking at the grey, sunless holiday snaps of happier years.

Saturday: Down to the Dymchurches' place for the week-end, with Reggie, Arthur Wissop, Eddie Nockstruck, and some of the Bewers-Loadwater crowd. Over lunch Arthur says the situation is even more serious than we

183

suppose – he has private information that 1964 is also the 225th anniversary of the War of Jenkin's Ear.

Eddie suggests that there might still be a chance to avoid it, if the Government took the bold step of going over to the duodecimal system, which would make it only the 189th anniversary.

'That would merely postpone the evil day, Eddie,' said Reggie wisely. 'We should soon be landed with the 200th duodecimal anniversary. You have to face up to these things one way or another.'

Eddie began to mutter something under his breath. 'What was that?' asked Reggie sharply. 'I said it's exactly 2,182 years since the outbreak of the Second Punic War,' replied Eddie. 'Why aren't you worrying about that?'

'Dammit, Eddie,' said Reggie coldly, 'there are *some* rules in this game.'

Sunday: Gathered around the Dymchurches' television set after dinner to watch for the latest bulletins. A queer, tense atmosphere. After the news Huw Wheldon broadcasts to the nation. 'It is my duty to inform you,' he says, his voice almost breaking, 'of two grave new developments in the situation. It is now clear that this year is the 140th anniversary of the First Burmese War, and the 125th anniversary of the China War of 1839. We must all be ready for celebrations at any moment.'

After the broadcast we sit in silence for some minutes, each absorbed in his own thoughts. Then Reggie says levelly that we have a long haul ahead of us – he mentions among other things the centenary of the Franco–Prussian War in 1970, and the bicentenary of the American War of Independence in 1975. Eddie begins to say that he can see no earthly reason for commemorating the American War of Independence, since we lost it, but even his friends shout him down. I do not think he speaks for Britain in her new mood.

184

Monday: Spend the day on war memoir work, patrolling the streets recording the hours of sunshine, and looking for apparently ordinary men doing apparently ordinary things. Meet Guppy Trottle outside Boodle's. 'Do you realise,' he says, 'that it is now exactly twenty-four hours since this time yesterday?' Make a note of it. Seems of little meaning or consequence now, like everything else, but one knows how solid and significant it will appear when it is recalled twenty-five years hence.

Now then

My feeling that archaeology is not so much an exact science as a sort of high-class blind man's buff has been considerably fortified by the Knossos affair. Professor L. R. Palmer has just proved that Knossos in Crete was not, as had been supposed, the cradle of European civilisation, but simply another offshoot of the Mycenaean Empire on the Greek mainland.

Apparently Sir Arthur Evans, who excavated Knossos, grossly misreported what he found, and as a result dated it all some two hunded years too early. Even leaving misreporting aside, the archaeological evidence from which the course of prehistory is deduced is dark, ambiguous stuff. One of the clues which put Professor Palmer on the trail in the Knossos case, for example, was a sentence in a Minoan Linear B script from another site which had previously been translated as 'Aigeus the Cretan brought it' but which he amended after further study of the handwriting to 'of Cretan workmanship with goats' head handles'.

You can see the difficulties facing archaeologists by imagining what they will conclude when, 2,000 years from now, they dig down through the hundred feet of soil which covered Britain after the Great Nuclear War in 1965, and excavate what turns out to be the remains of your house. Professor Snodgrass's report runs (as closely as it will go in English):

The excavation was our first glimpse into that period of prehistory about which almost nothing is known, the

186

Neoplastic Age. Although only a few fragments of the site were intact, we were fortunate enough to find several letter-containers (not unlike our modern envelopes) obviously addressed to the Neoplastic occupant of the site, which established his identity as a man called On Her Majesty's Service.

On Her Majesty's Service, or On as he was probably called for short, was clearly a priest, and the building he occupied a temple. Several things point to this – particularly the steel box found in one of the chambers which contained the mummified remains of offerings to the gods – the severed leg of a sheep and the carcase of a chicken, both of which seemed to have been subjected to some ritual treatment by fire. The box also contained an exquisitely worked glass container, presumably for holding holy oil, inscribed in raised letters with the magical rubric 'United Dairies'.

In one of the chambers we found a letter that On had kept in its original envelope, which suggests he placed some considerable value on it. Professor Grabowski, our philologist, has been unable so far to translate it exactly, but the address at the top is clearly a town called Income Tax in the province of Demand Note.

Our most valuable find was perhaps that of the holy texts used in the temple – four enormous, closely printed volumes of verse in head-rhyme. They are as yet imperfectly understood, but Professor Grabowski believes he has isolated a primitive creation legend in one of them. The first few lines are reproduced below. (The expressions in the righthand column are probably responses to be made by the congregation as the priest read aloud):

A1 Adhesives Ltd, Arlington
  Avenue Wks, Arlington Av., N1   CANonbry 7126
A1 Bureau, 66 Peckham Rd, SE5   RODney 4581
A1 Café, 299 Borough High St, SE1   HOP 3294

There is no doubt about where the rites were performed – a small chamber set apart as a holy of holies, big enough for only the priest to enter. The central object in the chamber is a hollowed-out altar, about waist-high, and made of white porcelain. To it are affixed a pair of metal figurines representing seated gods, one inscribed with the name 'Hot', the other 'Cold'.

It was perhaps fanciful, but as we stood in that holy place it required but little imagination to see before us On Her Majesty's Service, one of the last Neoplastic men, offering up a sheep's leg to the implacable Hot and Cold, chanting the endless litany of the Post Office Telephone Directory (London Postal Area), as the congregation in the outer chamber roared forth 'CANonbry 7126 ... RODney 4581 ... HOP 3294 ...' It is of such moments of insight as these that the stuff of archaeology is woven.

A farewell to arms

I'm glad the Pope's against war. Because so am I, and so is Horace Morris, and so are quite a number of other people I know.

The Pope and I don't always see eye to eye, but I'm bound to admit that on this one I think he's got hold of the right end of the stick. 'No more war, war never again . . .' as he told the assembled delegates at the UN. 'If you wish to be brothers, let the arms fall from your hands.' It touched a chord. In fact, judging by the headlines and the discussions on television, it seems to have evoked widespread acknowledgement and admiration, and no disagreement at all.

All the same, I think it is only fair to point out that the Pope was not the first to declare himself in favour of peace. The previous week very similar views were expressed by Mr Patrick McGoohan, described as Britain's highest-paid television actor, in an interview in *TV Times*.

Mr McGoohan was being interviewed by Iain Sproat (who, the *TV Times* was careful to point out, was educated at Winchester and Oxford, so you can be pretty sure he got it down right). 'We were once talking,' writes Mr Sproat, 'about the totally hypothetical question of what he would do were he Prime Minister. I remember he said nothing for a moment, and then: -

"I would be overwhelmed with fear, but if I were, I would try to get everyone to cease combat just for one minute. Just peace on earth for one minute! It's a fairy tale but you never know. It would feel so good that they might not start again."'

Harold Wilson must be kicking himself. Not once does it seem to have occurred to him to arrange a trial run of peace on earth! That's why they pay Mr McGoohan so much as an actor – to keep him out of politics.

Now I'm not for a moment accusing the Pope of lifting Mr McGoohan's ideas. I don't suppose he even set eyes on a copy of last week's *TV Times*. By some fluke Mr McGoohan missed the headlines – 'MCGOOHAN CALLS FOR PEACE ON EARTH,' 'CEASE COMBAT, URGES HIGHEST-PAID TV ACTOR' – and the Pope collected all the glory for much the same idea. Like Darwin and Wallace discovering evolution. Just one of those coincidences.

'Hasn't this peace business been around before?' asked my friend Horace Morris, as we sat discussing the history of ideas, in the way we often do. 'Weren't there some rather scruffy people you and I knocked around with in our youth who used to walk about the roads every Easter saying roughly, in effect, let the arms fall from your hands?'

'You mean the Aldermaston marchers?'

'That's right. Very statesmanlike of them, one realises now. Tremendous sense of moral leadership they were showing.'

'Good heavens, Horace, that was a different matter altogether! They were just a bunch of vague, muddle-headed idealists!'

'Not statesmanlike at all?'

'Certainly not. They weren't making a broad appeal to the hearts and minds of mankind – they were trying to get our own Government to disarm! That's politics, Horace. We'd have weakened our strategic posture against Communist intimidation.'

'But haven't the Communists been coming out for peace themselves recently, in a rather broad, statesmanlike way?'

'Broadish, I suppose, Horace. But what the Communists

mean by peace is peace in circumstances favourable to the spread of Communist ideas and influence.'

'Whereas the Pope means peace in circumstances favourable to the spread of anti-Communist ideas and influence?'

'I should think that's what he means, Horace. He doesn't specify, of course – he's had the sense not to get bogged down in particularities and details. But I don't suppose he means "Let the arms fall from your hands, and let the Communists peacefully take over South-East Asia." There's peace and peace, as I'm sure the Pope would be the first to recognise.'

'What he's telling us is "Let the arms fall from your hands, but go on defending freedom against tyranny and the rule of law against lawlessness"?'

'As it were.'

'By virtue as it were of the tyrants and outlaws responding to this broad supranational appeal too?'

'Exactly, as it were.'

'He sees both sides of the question?'

'I think seeing both sides of the question is his strong point, Horace. For instance, you remember he said he was against birth control?'

'I was a little worried by that, I must admit.'

'Ah, yes, but at the same time, Horace, he came out very strongly against people going hungry.'

'I see what you mean. The broad view? The bipartisan approach?'

'Quite. In fact, he advised people to make new efforts to increase the world's food supply. Rather a bright idea, don't you think?'

'I see what you mean. Really, short of doing anything it lies in his power to do, like changing his mind about birth control, he's doing everything he can.'

The faith of a snout baron

It must have been a moving moment when Lord Sinclair of Cleeve, the tobacco baron, stood up in the House of Lords during the debate on smoking and said he wanted to 'refute conclusively some of the baser allegations made against the reputation of an industry which I have been proud to serve.'

I wonder how many people had realised before that the tobacco industry was an institution which men were proud to serve, and which had a reputation they were prepared to stand up and defend against dishonour? I'm not sure that the industry shouldn't make the facts more widely known – perhaps commission a film about life in the tobacco industry which brought out something of its essential nobility. But why should I be modest? Gentlemen, I have the scenario you want right here:-

Handsome, dashing young Simon Ricepaper, scion of one of the oldest and proudest tobacco families in the land, who has passed out of the Royal Tobacco Academy top in smoke-ring blowing and winner of the Cigarette-holder of Honour, joins a crack Kingsizer company.

As the youngest member of the board-room here he has to undergo all the time-honoured initiation pranks and rituals of the Company, and in these his chief tormentor is the board-room madcap, Freddie Twenty. Simon despairs of ever being accepted by his fellow directors. But one day, when Freddie and Simon are leading a detachment sent out to bring a tribe of blackamoors in a remote colony under

192

the cigarette, Freddie gets cut off and surrounded by dangerous anti-smoking killjoys. Simon goes to help him, fearlessly bombarding the killjoys with any arguments that come to hand. 'Fwightfully decent of you to wescue me like that,' drawls Freddie as together they manage to evade the issue. From then on Simon and Freddie are fast friends.

But at the next board-room dining-in night, Simon is in trouble again. Colonel Flake, the Chairman, is holding forth about the Great Sales Drive of '53, when the Company massacred over a thousand smokers in one campaign. Simon, exhausted after advertising practice, falls asleep. One of his fellow-directors, dark, saturnine Rupert de Luxe, draws Colonel Flake's attention to it, and Simon is given an extra two weeks as duty director.

Instead of enjoying himself at the annual Company ball the following week, therefore, Simon has to be at his post, ready to deal promptly with any outbreak of non-smoking in the Company's distribution area. It is here that lovely Virginia Flake, the Chairman's daughter and the toast of the board-room, finds him when, filled with a strange melancholy, she slips away from the brilliant throng within. All his chivalry aroused, Simon offers her a cigarette, and she tells him she is engaged to Rupert de Luxe. But when their eyes meet, they both know that the curling blue ribbons of smoke from their cigarettes are hopelessly entwined.

But Simon's trials are still not over. The very next day, as Simon offers Colonel Flake his cigarette-case in the ante-room, the monocle slips from the Chairman's eye. 'Cork-tipped!' he exclaims, going white with anger. 'This is an insult which I should never have expected to see bandied about between Kingsizers, Ricepaper. Kindly have your papers in my hands by the morning.'

Simon accepts the sentence stoically, although he knows it was not he who filled his case with the cowardly cork tips.

As soon as they are safely outside, Freddie cries: 'It's that cad Wupert de Luxe! I saw him at your cigawette-case while you were out last night!'

Simon accuses de Luxe, who challenges him to a duel. Simon chooses to fight with cigarettes, and they slog it out behind the fives court, swapping puff for puff for twelve hours before de Luxe, wheezing and gasping, cries: 'I give in! I don't want to die! I confess everything. I planted the cork tips on you because I didn't want a rival for Virginia – and her father's money! And you may as well know that I'm a deserter from the Woodbine Corps.'

'I just did what I had to do,' says Simon modestly, one arm round Virginia, the other being fervently shaken by Colonel Flake, 'for the honour of the Company and the good name of tobacco.'

'Bwavo!' cries loyal Freddie, 'and here's a telegwam to say that thwee of the customers you were wesponsible for have died of lung cancer. Blooded at last, Simon – now you're weally one of us!'

The bar sinister

According to usually reliable gossip columns, considerable efforts are being made to clean up the Hotel Petersberg, outside Bonn, where the Queen will stay on her visit to Germany. Apparently they're taking down 'all the usual hotel signs, such as *bar* and *toilet*'.

Experts have long known about the suggestiveness of the word 'toilet', of course. Which of us, indeed, has not crept past the sign in some lewd five-star hotel, his eyes averted, a crimson blush mantling his cheek for very shame?

The obscene connotations of the word 'bar' for the moment elude me, I must admit. *Bar* . . . BAR . . . No, I don't quite get the full lascivious frisson. I see the objections to 'public bar', of course; the L might drop out of 'public' just as the Queen walked by. There's something vaguely indecent about 'saloon bar', too – I think it's the combination of the *sal* of 'salacious' with the *oon* of 'spittoon'.

I'm sure there's no need to mention what the 'private' parts of 'private bar' call to mind for a person of sensitivity. As for 'c-cktail bar', I'm astonished that it has ever been allowed, even in places where only commoners would see it. How many perfectly common folk must have staggered back in astonishment and disgust from the 'c-tktail bar' sign, only to find themselves among the tasteless liberties of the Off Licence?

I've just seen what's wrong with 'BAR'. Heh, heh, heh! Hnuh, hnuh, hnuh! Got it? No? Boys, there's a feller here who can't see anything dirty in the word 'BAR'! Shnuh, shnuh, shnuh!

No? All right, I'll take pity on your simplicity. Stand well back from the page. Close one eye, and screw up the other until everything begins to look fuzzy. Now, look at the word ' BAR'. Got it? The A and the R appear to change places, so that the word seems to read 'BRA'! If that's not an indecent announcement I don't know what is. Some member of the royal party, returning after a hard day's hand-shaking, screwing up their eyes in the sudden twinkle of lights behind the Campari bottles, might easily get it smack across their consciousness.

Did I say C-mpari bottles? Correction; all the alleged C-mpari bottles will have been hidden in the cellars. On display in the bar there'll be nothing but a lot of Bols. Sorry – a lot of B-ls is just what there won't be. I mean brandy. What? Brandy spelt b. randy? Curaçao and curaçao! They'll be shouting for large highballs next.

Now, wait a moment. You may think it doesn't matter all that much what the Queen sees or doesn't see. Do you know the story about the Labouchère Amendment, which first made male homosexual behaviour a criminal offence? According to the reforming journals I read, it was originally drafted to include female homosexuality as well. But when they showed it to Queen Victoria she objected on the grounds that female homosexuality was impossible, and since no one had the courage to enlighten her, the amendment became only half as brutal as had been intended.

Now had the Queen enjoyed a *really* pure upbringing, and not been allowed to catch glimpses of signs saying 'Public Conveniences' as she forayed forth among her people, she wouldn't have known that male homosexuality was on the cards, either, and the whole amendment would have been frustrated.

But back to the Hotel Petersberg. Did I tell you that the word 'service' is being deleted from the Queen's bill, in view of its connotation in the field of animal husbandry?

They're taking all the numbers off the doors, too. They started with the sixes, since 'six' in German is *sechs* (they're much more outspoken about these things on the Continent). Afterwards the Palace said they weren't too happy about *elf, zwölf*, or *zwanzig*, either. Just a feeling that there might be something a bit off-colour here if they'd known more German.

Then they admitted frankly that they weren't entirely easy in their minds about *fünf, acht* and *neun*. And then they thought, hell, in for a penny, in for a pound – why have naked figures prancing about the corridors at all? By the time the royal party arrives the whole hotel will be in a very decent state. All through the livelong night gentlemen will be stealing along the passages trying the anonymous doors, searching for the t--l-t, and bursting instead by mistake into the rooms of unchaperoned single ladies.

The unchaperoned single ladies, I trust, will scream in discreet tones about their h-n--r, and flee in their delectable diaphanous nightgowns to seek sanctuary in the M-n-g-r's Office. By a pardonable error in the circumstances, they will almost certainly rush headlong into the G-ntl-m-n's L-v-t-ry, where a merry party will be in occupation already, leaning their elbows on the washbasins and knocking back glass after glass of water, shouting 'Set 'em up again, b-rm-n!' and selling each other potash concessions in Eastern Bohemia.

Meanwhile, sitting round the extraordinary vast green table with six pockets in what they erroneously take to be the R-st--r-nt, the royal party waits patiently for dinner to appear . . .

The literature of coexistentialism

The last time I was in Moscow an article I wrote for the *Guardian* describing my impressions of that city called forth half a column of personal abuse in *Izvestia*, in which I was described as 'a stinking rocket of the Cold War'. So I was delighted to find this week a model of the sort of article I should have written – a piece by Mr Alexei Adzhubei, the editor-in-chief of *Izvestia*, on his impressions of London.

The article was written at the request of the *Sunday Express*, after Mr Adzhubei had visited Britain for the unofficial talks at Wiston House (and incidentally offered to take over the editorial chair of the *Daily Mail* and double the paper's readership in two months). When the *Sunday Express* saw the finished product, however, they turned it down, on the grounds that it did not 'quite measure up to the standard of interest and entertainment that we aim to provide'.

It was rescued from the waste-paper basket by the *Sunday Pictorial*, who published it together with a reproach for the 'puny and frivolous' attitude of the *Sunday Express* towards the problem of understanding the Russians.

Just how considerable this problem is you can discover for yourself by reading Mr Adzhubei's article. I will make my little contribution to solving it by admitting that by Adzhubei standards my piece on Moscow was simply not up to scratch. Humbly confessing my past errors, I present it again, entirely rewritten in the the peaceful coexistence style. *Izvestia* may reprint it if they want to, but if it doesn't quite measure up to their standard of interest and entertainment I'll submit it for the 'What I did in my holidays' competition in *Chicks' Own*.

MOSCOW

Moscow is an interesting city. I am happy to have the opportunity of describing my impressions of it. Perhaps this is because it is such an interesting city. Or perhaps there is some other explanation.

I will be as brief as possible. I must say first that we in England have already heard of your city. It is, in my opinion, a big city. There are many buildings and streets in it. I do not want to trespass on your countrymen's most intimate national feelings, but as I walked round the streets I could not help thinking, 'This is a big city, and it is an interesting one.'

In a short article like this there is not enough space to list all the sights I saw. But I must mention the Kremlin, an old building which I find most interesting. I also saw Red Square and the Bolshoi Theatre. I don't have to tell you that, by and large, and on whole, they are impressive and interesting. There were also many other sights of historical interest I saw in Moscow. I have no space to mention them all, but as I looked at them I was most strongly impressed by how interesting they were. Need I add that some of them were also big?

While I was in Moscow I heard Russian spoken. It was spoken by Russians, quite fluently. To all you Russians, whether in Moscow, Leningrad, Kiev, or Odessa, I bring greetings from the people of London, Manchester, Birmingham, and Bury St Edmunds. I talked to some of you about subjects too numerous to mention here. We did not attempt to listen to one another. Everyone must decide for himself how to live, without listening to anyone else.

199

Unless the editor has any objection, I should like to give some more of my impressions of Moscow, although space is too limited to mention more than a few. I saw cars and buses in the streets. I saw trains going along by the ingenious use of wheels running on rails. All this is the Moscow one does not read about in guide books. I find it very interesting.

Very soon now there won't be any more space left before the end of the article. I should like to use what there is to say that even if there were more space left, which there is not, I rather doubt if I could have given a better impression of your big and interesting town. To sum up, I saw the Kremlin, Red Square, the Bolshoi Theatre, and many other historical monuments which lack of space prevents me mentioning by name. On this note I must conclude my article, which I am writing on paper, sitting at a table.

Rabarbaro, rabarbaro

If statistics (those venal rhetoricians) do not lie, the majority of Englishmen who go abroad for their summer holidays end up in Italy. It is about this time of year that they come face to face with the annual question of whether or not this time they are going to make some effort to master the melodious subtleties of the Italian language before they go.

For years I didn't. I relied on the titles of Italian films and the endless, patient sympathy of the Italian people, who seemed to be able to make some sense of my *instruzione* about the *rectificazione* of the *carburazione* and the like. Then a couple of years ago I did a whirlwind tour through the first few lessons of the excellent EUP *Teach Yourself Italian.* All I can remember now is that it dealt extensively with the whereabouts and activities of *la cuoca* (the cook) and *il postino* (the postman). What, people were always asking, was the cook doing? Where, the cry was for ever going up, was the postman? And the answer would come that they were dallying together in the Via Tornabuoni. It was always the Via Tornabuoni.

My studies were cut short by scoring such an instant linguistic bulls-eye in Italy that further effort seemed superfluous. A girl asked me to get her some mucilage of tragacanth, and I got it. (I just said to the chemist: 'Hast thou a thing to stick the hairs of a signorina?' and the first thing that wise and kindly man took down from his shelf was mucilage of tragacanth, clairvoyant as it may seem.)

Now my interest has been stirred again by a man in

201

Coventry, who has sent me the following vocabulary, culled from the *Cambridge Shorter Italian Dictionary*:

Nipotame: Crowd of nephews and nieces.
Ganascino, dare il: To pinch the cheek of a child using the back of the fingers.
Palleggiare: To toss a baby about.
Baffona: Woman with a not unpleasing moustache.
Tra le due selle: Middle-sized horse, woman neither pretty nor plain.
Buzzo: Paunch, person capable of any iniquity.
Sbuzzare: To stab in the belly, to open a parcel not addressed to oneself.
Sfognare: To fall into or emerge from a sewer.
Loffa: Silent discharge of wind.

Italian is clearly a language worth studying further, if only because Italian literature must practically write itself. Even with the materials to hand already we have a play virtually made. Pedestrian in English, it would go into Italian like a knife into butter.

> *Scene: The Via Tornabuoni. Enter the* COOK *and the* POSTMAN.

POSTMAN (romantically):	You have a by no means unpleasing moustache.
COOK (simpering):	Oh, I'm just a middle-sized horse, neither pretty nor plain.
POSTMAN:	From one end of the Via Tornabuoni to the other there is no one with such a not unpleasing moustache as you. I will give you an indicazione of my affezione.

Look in my mailbag and stab in the belly a parcel not addressed to yourself!

(While the COOK *is stabbing, a crowd of nephews and nieces enters. The* POSTMAN *pinches their cheeks, using the back of his fingers since with the front of them he is amorously pinching the* COOK. *When he has finished this he tosses a baby about. Enter the baby's* MOTHER.)*

MOTHER: That baby you were tossing about has fallen into a sewer!

(Uproar. A CROWD *forms, muttering 'Rabarbaro, rabarbaro. [Roughly, 'Rhubarb, Rhubarb.'])*

CROWD (shouting at postman): You paunch, capable of any iniquity!

MOTHER OF THE BABY (at last making herself heard over the noise):

Stop! It's all a linguistic ambiguity! When I said the baby had fallen into a sewer, what I meant was that it had *emerged* from a sewer.

(Sensazione. Jubilazione. The COOK *succeeds in stabbing open the parcel which is not addressed to her, and pulls forth some mucilage of tragacanth.)*

COOK (ecstatically): What a divine comedy!

(She kisses the POSTMAN, *and is instantly arrested for public indecency. The* POSTMAN, *invited by reporters to make a statement, emits a silent discharge of wind.)*

Fine

(The heaviest you can impose, your worship.)

51 to Blangy

Another kilometre stone coming up ... 51 to Blangy-le-Duc. Superb views on either side of the road, any of which we could stop and look at if we chose. Delightful sensation of being captain of one's own destiny. Muse on therapeutic effect car has on human ego. One's choice potential is extended, and ... Become conscious of wife asking question. Stop musing. Listen.

'*... just thinking why don't we stop along here somewhere and look at the view?*'

Stop? Of course. Could easily, anywhere. With so many superb views, only difficulty to know where. Not *there*, obviously – right next to electric pylon. And not *there*, clearly – two cars there already. Now a very narrow bit with nowhere to pull off the road. Just get this stretch over and look again.

Now, slow. That spot would have been all right anywhere else, but not quite as good as some of the places we passed a mile or two back. What's that hooting behind? Good God, lorry I overtook five minutes ago trying to overtake me! Damned liberty! If I go back to my normal speed, like this, you'll realise what a big mistake you're making, my friend.

'*That looked quite a good place.*'

'What? Oh, I didn't see it. Not worth going back, is it?'

Rather dull stretch here. Kilometre post coming up. Still 48 kilometres to Blangy-le-Duc. Hm. Now 11.30, so must have been averaging scarcely 60 kilometres an hour since St-Sévère. If it's the same sort of road ahead, that means we shan't be at Blangy until about 12.15. Then it's about, say, 70 kilometres from Blangy to Le Hoquet – say, 1.30. Then, say, half an hour for . . .

'*Aren't you going to stop, then?*'

'Um? Stop?'

. . . half an hour for lunch. Say two o'clock. Then round about 100 kilometres from Le Hoquet to Pisaller. Say . . .

'*To look at the view.*'

'What view? Rather seedy bit here.'

. . . say four o 'clock, allowing a bit of time in hand, which will give us about two hours to get down to Uze . . .

'*Perhaps we ought to stop in Blangy instead, then.*'

'Is there something we ought to see there?'

'*Fifteenth-century castle, Romanesque cathedral, musée gastronomique, and traditional slipper-weaving industry.*'

Just a moment, what does that kilometre stone say? Blangy 45. Must stop looking at kilometre stones. Tedious obsession. Still, done those three kilometres in just under three minutes. If we kept that up we'd make Blangy at say 12.05, and Le Hoquet at . . .

'*What do you think?*'

'What? Oh, yes. Yes.'

. . . Le Hoquet at, say, 1.15. Though not if we're stopping at Blangy, of course. Forgotten that. Throws the whole calculation right out.

'We don't want to stop very long at Blangy, do we?'

'*We ought to look at it for a bit, oughtn't we?*'

Let's see. Say 10 minutes for the Romanesque cathedral, 10 minutes for the museum, five minutes for the castle – oh, say about 30 minutes altogether. Here's another kilometre stone coming up. Won't look this time. Well, perhaps just this once. Forty-three! Two kilometres in two and a half minutes! That means we shan't be at Blangy until about 12.20, and if we stop for half an hour, that means 2.10, no, 2.20 at Le Hoquet and . . . Must explain all this carefully to wife.

'I was just thinking, we don't really want to look round a museum in this heat, do we? What do you think?'

'What do you think?'

Cut the museum, then. After all, we've got 170 solid kilometres to do between Blangy and Pisaller. What's that in miles? Multiply by eight and divide by five: 270 miles. 270 miles! God, it can't be! Can it?

'I was thinking, perhaps we ought to give the traditional bedsock factory a miss. After all, we did spend at least half an hour looking round Cahiers yesterday. No one could accuse us of – well, I don't know, whatever anyone might start accusing us of. What do you think?'

'I don't know. What do you think?'

Cut the bedsock works, then. That saves us, what, 15 minutes? So we should reach Le Hoquet at . . . Did I say 270 miles? I must have meant 170 miles, or 270 kilometres. Mustn't I? Still, either way . . .

'We saw a Romanesque cathedral yesterday at Cahiers, didn't we?'

'Did we? I thought it was a Gothic bell-tower we saw at Cahiers.'

Gothic bell-tower . . . ? Watch out, another kilometre stone coming up. No, no! Must stop looking at the damn things!

'Perhaps you'd rather not stop at Blangy at all?'

'Of course we must stop there. We don't want to go charging across the country without ever seeing anything, do we? We're not in a charabanc. It's just that I don't want to spend the whole damned holiday looking at Romanesque cathedrals, that's all . . .'

'Two in ten days is scarcely . . .'

'Two? What was that thing we drove past in the rain at Grince? Wasn't that a Romanesque cathedral?'

Have to stop at Blangy for petrol, anyway. Will it see us through the 270 kilometres to Pisaller if we get 20 litres, plus the gallon and a half in the tank now, less the 40 kilometres from here to Blangy at 38 miles per gallon? Let's see, 20 divided by about 42.5, plus or minus 40 times 5 divided by 8 multiplied by 38. No, no . . .

'*Look out!*'

'All right, all right. I could see him perfectly well, I assure you.'

I suppose if it's a fifteenth-century castle . . . Perhaps we could just find a petrol station where we could see the castle without getting out of the car. Now, say we stopped for 10 minutes. In English minutes, that's 10 times 5 over 8, say 61 minutes. Or do I mean 16 kilominutes? If I could just work that out in cathedrals per litre . . .

Heart-cry from beautiful Yvonne Romaine

It was pure chivalry which stayed my hand in the act of consigning to the waste-paper basket a publicity handout entitled *The Curse of the Werewolf*, News Sheet No 3. My eye, usually afflicted by temporary blindness at the sight of a handout, had caught the headline 'Heart-Cry From Beautiful Yvonne Romaine'. Whipping out my Boy Scout penknife, which has an attachment for helping maidens in distress, I quickly read on. The piteous complaint welling up from the tortured depths of Miss Romaine's heart turned out to be: 'I Always Seem To Be More Corpse Than Cutie!'

Here was a girl in trouble and no mistake. She had played a corpse in *Circus of Horrors*, explained News Sheet No 3, hurled herself to destruction over a cliff in *Interpol*, and been shot dead in *Danger Man*. Now beautiful twenty-two-year-old Yvonne Romaine is acting in *The Curse of the Werewolf*, and she really seems to have reached the end of the line. She plays the part of a deaf-mute girl who dies in childbirth after being delivered of a werewolf cub. 'I confess,' she lisps fetchingly, 'I froze like an ice-cube when I started reading the script.'

I have nothing but sympathy – unlike her so-called friends. This stony hearted bunch, according to News Sheet No 3, find Miss Romaine's tendency to freeze like an ice-cube 'strange', pointing out with what passes for logic in their part of the world that she is half Maltese and

208

combines the earthy beauty of Magnano with the smouldering fire of Loren. Goodness me, I've known earthy, smouldering folk, pure-blooded Maltese on both sides of the family, who fainted dead away at the mere sight of a werewolf.

'No,' she says in answer to the question hovering on the lips of a thousand journalists, 'I cannot really explain my fear of the macabre. I am not naturally nervous. I am not afraid of heights, high speeds, or stunting in airplanes. I'm not morally uncourageous.' Except to add that she is married to a man who 'feeds comedy lines and gags to distinguished funsters', that seems more or less to complete the case history of Miss Yvonne Romaine.

Aunty Frayn replies:

Dear Yvonne,

Troubles never come singly, do they, my dear? But I'm sure the dark days will not last for ever, and that your moral courage and your fearless readiness for stunting in airplanes will win through to a brighter dawn ahead.

I know how difficult it is, believe me, when one feels one is more corpse than cutie. But it's no good fretting, my dear. Some of us are born to be cuties, and some to be corpses. No man whose love is worth anything at all will turn away from you simply because you are a corpse. And you can improve your appearance tremendously, you know, by the use of a good embalming fluid.

As for your other trouble, I am putting you in touch with a society which exists to help girls in just your position. It seems a pity you are dying in childbirth, though, for you will not have the opportunity to live down your moment of weakness in the years of selfless work for others which I usually recommend. A werewolf cub can be great fun, you know, and I am sending you under separate cover a book entitled *The Complete Practical Werewolf Breeder*. Perhaps after you are gone your

209

husband will rally round. Try to persuade him to cease feeding gags to distinguished funsters and start feeding the werewolf instead.

New man coming

One's personality is a remarkably stable structure; and the most stable element in it is one's steadfast conviction that it is just on the point of being entirely transformed.

Transformed, needless to say, not by any efforts of one's own, but by magic objects and events outside oneself. One's dissatisfactions and limitations will be suddenly and wonderfully sloughed off, one comes to believe, when one has acquired a striped suit, or a red car; when one has got married; when one has written a book, or found God, or learnt Italian; when one has reached the age of ten; when one has moved house; when summer comes.

It is strange that so much of one's action is motivated by such patent witchcraft. But in a society where unhappiness is regarded rather like fleas, as an unappealing state that people ought to be ashamed of getting into, I suppose it is congenial to see oneself as a naturally happy soul hindered from achieving perfect contentment only by external causes. All these extraordinary superstitions are ways of concealing from oneself the painful fact that most of one's discontents are the inevitable by-products of one's own nature.

I rely a bit on almost all these superstitions, but most particularly on those that involve straightforward covetousness. If I had a certain material object, I have repeatedly felt, my whole life would be entirely changed. From its small corner the totem would radiate such a powerful field of rightness and delight that everything else would come to glow in sympathy.

The first thing I can remember coveting as a child was a propelling pencil that wrote in five colours, after I had seen the teacher correcting exercise books with one. Other little boys might have conceived a passion for the teacher, but I fell in love with the propelling pencil. It was beautiful, and I desired it. The provocative glimpses of the coloured leads through the slots in the side inflamed my senses. I longed to touch the exquisite texture of the nickel-plating.

My parents were driven to say they would buy me one – but, torment of hopes raised only to be the more savagely hurled down, there was none in the shops! I raged about the house like a tiny junkie deprived of his fix, while they ransacked London, and after days of great misery for all of us, ran one to earth in far-off Peckham Rye. But so supremely unimportant did it become as soon as I possessed it that I cannot even remember what happened to it.

It sometimes seems to me that the whole story of my life could be adequately told in the catalogue of these love affairs. There was the affair with the ten-and-sixpenny plastic crystal set (purchased – never worked); the affair with the miniature starting-pistol (owned by a friend – fiercely desired through long centuries of time – swapped for about half my possessions – instantly devalued, and allowed to fall to pieces before it could fire the five blank cartridges which my friend's father was keeping locked up to celebrate the end of the war with); the affair with the second-hand sports car (£180 – 'Take you anywhere, that car,' said the salesman. 'Take you to Land's End and back'), snatched away at the last moment by a providential failure to raise the money.

One learns, of course. I don't think I shall ever fall in love with another propelling pencil, or another plastic crystal set. But the inoculation is against the particular ju-jus I've tried, not against ju-jus in general. It doesn't in any way deter me from my present mania, for example, which is
212

coveting a swivel chair. If I had a swivel chair, upholstered in worn leather, I know I should be a new man.

I can see myself very clearly with the swivel chair. I am a calm man, a responsible man, a happy man, a man who can work for eight hours at a stretch without being interrupted by fatigue, boredom, bad temper or incompetence, a man who can take well-earned relaxation with his smiling wife and laughing child in some agreeable but uplifting leisure pursuit. I am a man who keeps an exquisitely selected early June day permanently outside his window. I am a man who does not get telephone calls from people who think they are phoning the South Eastern Gas Board.

I am a man who is swinging gently from side to side in his worn leather swivel chair as he decides whether to spend the sunlit working day ahead on finishing his play about the ultimate essence of man, or starting the essay in which the ultimate nature of the universe is set forth in 500 exact and simple words.

Manufacturers of swivel chairs, join me in happy contemplation of the picture! Sooner or later I shall have the swivel chair, and you will have the money for it. How would you sell me a swivel chair I do not need if I did not believe I was buying a complete new personality? How would any five-colour propelling pencils ever be sold if other people did not share my disorder? How would the evangelists and travel agents survive?

And just as surely as I know that the man in the swivel chair will be a new and perfect man, so I know he will be the same inadequate one, not only depressed by the weather, interrupted by the telephone, unable to find a pen that works, and confused about exactly what he is supposed to be doing, but also driven to final exasperation because the swivel on the blasted chair is broken.

I know it only too well. Perhaps it's just as well for all concerned that I don't actually believe it.

My life and loves

Distinguished civil servants and others, when they realise they are being observed by a journalist, hastily leap up from their armchairs and with rather unexpected quiet passion and rather unexpectedly engaging smiles begin to play badminton, collect seventeenth-century Irish egg-whisks, write the standard work on the lesser celandine, reveal a rather unexpected line in wry humour, take a rather unexpectedly serious interest in the campaign to preserve the death-watch beetle, and beget ten rather brilliant children; continuing this dazzling simultaneous exhibition until the journalist leaves, when (I should imagine) they slump heavily back into their armchairs rather unexpectedly exhausted.

The behaviour of distinguished actors and actresses when a journalist or handout writer comes over the horizon is entirely different. They don't start *doing* anything at all They just start believing in and being intensely moved by and being utterly realistic about. They simply come vibrantly, richly, and passively into contact with life.

Here, for instance, is the throbbing voice of an actress called Yvette Mimieux in a newspaper cutting I have: 'I like snails and hot chocolate and dancing and tangy cheese and soft lead pencils and thick, strong coffee and tangerines and racing cars.'

Imagine the Permanent Secretary at the Ministry of Waste Disposal taking this sort of line. '"I adore walking in the rain," lisped Mr O. R. Strood, the tough-minded *éminence grise* behind Britain's newest rubbish tip, "and the smell of new bread and comfortably worn dispatch-boxes and thinking and Ministry cars and mid-morning biscuits and chewing my pencil and – oh – heaps of things."' Be rather unexpected, to say the least.

But it looked perfectly natural when Mr Nicol Williamson, actor, listed his loves to Mr Marshall Pugh, journalist, in the *Daily Mail* last week. Mr Williamson, it appears, loves old wooden houses, Bach, good stew and ale, pubs, belting tennis balls about, and diving into the sea and coming back and scattering his records all over the room.

How he stands on hot chocolate and tangy cheese and soft lead pencils he doesn't say. But he did come out for humility – 'I'm humble in some ways,' he told Mr Pugh, 'much humbler than you think' – and faith. 'Faith bothered him constantly,' reported Mr Pugh. 'It was so bloody personal, such bloody agony.'

Yes! Oh God, yes! Oh God, I absolutely bloody agree! The smell of coffee roasting, sunlight falling on hair, the clouds coming down on the mountains – I love them all, too. I may not have mentioned it before, but I'm involved in life up to my bloody eyebrows. Gregorian plainsong, hot, strong cheese and tangy snails – I'm deeply committed to every corny, wonderful, bloody experience in the book. I've never tried diving in the sea and coming back and scattering my records all over the room, but oh God, it sounds marvellous! I'll give it a whirl at the very first opportunity I have.

And there's the snag – opportunity. As Mr Williamson says: 'I want to live intensively, 101 per cent. But how can I do it in this job?'

God, I know the feeling! How can I do it, either, in my job, or you in yours? And if it's not the job stopping us living it's something else. Just as you're about to start living, really 101 per cent living, it's lunchtime. Or some damned person rings up. You get inside some lovable pub and you never

215

have a chance to really experience it, because you have to spend all the time either trying to break into your friends' conversation to ask them what they want to drink, or trying to catch the barmaid's eye.

And the hot chocolate – that turns up just when you feel like the thick, strong coffee, and the thick, strong coffee is wheeled on just about bedtime, when the only thing you want is hot chocolate. Nor is it possible to listen to the Bach properly when you're hunting high and low for something to write with, because all you can find is some damned joky soft lead pencil.

No, if you want to live – *really* live – you've got to get away from life. You've got to find somewhere where you can be completely idle, so that if you want to spend all morning walking in the rain you can, for the simple reason that there's nothing else to do. And if you happen to come across a smell of coffee roasting you can stop and inhale it – and go on inhaling it until you're fed up with it. Then you can sit down in a café somewhere and have a hot chocolate. Have two hot chocolates if you feel like it – there's nothing else to do. Go on guzzling hot chocolate until you're chocolate-coloured in the face. Then you can start walking about in the rain again, trying to get up an appetite for that lunch of stew and ale.

After lunch you could go and look at some wooden houses. Look at them from the front, look at them from the back. Really get an eyeful of them – there's no earthly hurry. Then perhaps you could stroll along and smell the coffee roasting again. Have another hot chocolate. If the weather's cleared up you might go and take a dive in the sea, then go up to your room and chuck the records about. After that you might go out and take another dive, and chuck the records about all over again – you've probably still got about four hours left before dinner . . .

No, if you're really going to live – really 101 per cent

live – you need some purpose in life. You need to work. Oh God, think of that bloody marvellous little pub you used to slip out to after a hard day's work! And the Goldberg Variations tinkling quietly away in the background as you worked with the soft lead pencil! Oh God, how bloody wonderful such moments are – in recollection, if you didn't think about them when they happened!

In Funland

Sigismund Cortex, that keen Psychomanian student of British affairs, is greatly excited by the idea of Miss Joan Littlewood's Fun Palace. The only trouble is, he can't understand exactly what a Fun Palace is.

He keeps alternately interrogating me and hunting through a stack of English–Psychomanian dictionaries. He says they have plenty of palaces in his country, but so far as he can tell they don't have any fun. I mean *I* know what a Fun Palace is, but it's damned difficult to explain it to *him*.

'Is a Palace of Culture?' he asks keenly.

'Not exactly,' I reply helpfully.

'Is a Palace of Varieties?'

'I don't think so.'

'Is a sports stadium?'

'Oh no.'

'Ah, now I see! Is a house of prostitution?'

'Certainly not.'

He turns some more pages in the dictionary.

'You see, Michael, it is important that we in our country keep up with the technologically more advanced nations. We refuse to be excluded from the comity of fun-loving nations. Now excuse me, please. I read in a newspaper that this Fun Palace would contain six-screen cinemas, mobile cycloramas, warm-air curtains, optical barriers and static-vapour zones. Tell me, please, are these the funs?'

'No, the fun's what goes on the screens and between the barriers.'

218

'Describe this fun, please.'

'Well, I don't think they've decided what sort of fun they're going to have in there yet.'

'No? They build the building first and then find the fun afterwards?'

'I think that's the idea, Sigismund.'

He suddenly finds a new word in the dictionary.

'Ah, now I understand!' he cries. 'Is a funfair!'

'I'm sure it's not. I'm sure it's dedicated to a much higher and broader concept of fun than that. You see, Sigismund, we have more and more fun in our country these days because we have more and more leisure to have fun in. What we believe now is that almost anything can be fun, if you go about it in the right spirit.'

'Almost anything?'

'If it's fun to do.'

'Aaaaaaaah! You *do* fun? Fun is something you *do*?'

'Oh no – fun's something you *have*.'

'Aaaaaaaah! You *have* fun! Like you have flu?'

'Exactly.'

'You mean, if this dictionary has fun I catch fun?'

'No, if the dictionary is, you have.'

'Excuse me, please. Where is the fun? In me or in the book?'

'I'm not absolutely sure.'

'But the book does not have fun?'

'Certainly not.'

Sigismund makes a careful note of these points.

'In Psychomania,' he says, 'we have sports, pastimes, amusements, diversions, hobbies and various erotic activities. We also have jokes and laughter. You know laughter? Laughter goes ha, ha, ha.'

'We have jokes and laughter in our country, too.'

'Ah! Now, is jokes and laughter fun?'

'Certainly. But fun isn't just jokes and laughter, you know.'

Sigismund starts to plough through the dictionary again, his eyes great pools of blankness.

'Look, Sigismund, the point is this. Nice things can be fun. But in this country we believe that nasty things can be fun, too. Mathematics can be fun. Culture can be fun. Even *work* can be fun.'

'Work can be fun?'

'Certainly. No man of real integrity in this country would dream of working if he didn't find it fun. Otherwise he'd just be selling out, wouldn't he? Why do you think the Prime Minister is slogging away up there in Downing Street?'

'Well, now, because he feels a patriotic duty to . . .'

'That's an unkind thing to say, Sigismund. I can assure you he does it simply because it's fun. Why do you think perfectly intelligent university graduates go into advertising?'

'Surely, because they are paid a lot of money . . .'

'Good heavens, Sigismund, you are a cynic! No, they do it because everyone knows advertising is tremendous fun. Why do you think Milton wrote that damned great poem of his? Because he was a fun person and it was a fun thing to do. "I had a lot of fun writing it," he told reporters, as you probably know, "and all I hope is that people have as much fun reading it."'

'He said that?'

'Certainly he did. We live in a fun culture, Sigismund. It's fun to dance till dawn in a topless dinner-jacket at the Reform Club. It's fun to get down on your hands and knees and scrub the floor with new magic Elbo-Grees.'

'Michael, this I never knew. But what are the symptoms of having fun?'

'Well, one finds oneself saying "Gosh, this is fun!" Or "Heavens, I am having fun!"'

'Excuse me, I make a note . . .'

'Yes, write it down, Sigismund. P-E-O-P-L-E A-R-E F-U-N. That's our great humanistic creed. It's fun to be alive. It's fun to drop dead.'

Smoothe's law

Of course, I'm entirely on the side of the nurses, God bless 'em (*said Rollo Swavely, the well-known public relations consultant*), but all this shindig about their pay has been damned unfair on Christopher Smoothe. I handle his private account, as you know, and I've seen the strain, the terrible sense of injustice, that he's been labouring under these last few weeks.

You see, Mike, everyone thinks it's rotten luck that nurses get five pounds a week, or five pounds a month, or whatever it is. And of course luck's the responsibility of Christopher, as Minister of Chance and Spec. It's not as if it was just the nurses – it's been civil servants, teachers, railwaymen – one after the other. 'What bad luck!' says everyone – and Christopher gets the blame once again. Well, he's just a human being like you and me, Mike. He can't help worrying about it.

That's why some time ago he set up this National Wages Explanation Council ('Nwexie' to you), under the chairmanship of Arthur Weefellow, the Professor of Ancient Economics at Twicester. It's not that he's for one moment doubting the fundamental Conservative principle of leaving all human affairs to the free operation of chance. But he believes fervently that all the Government's present difficulties can be solved by public relations, and as a genuinely constructive step in this direction he's given Nwexie the task of discovering some general principles that would explain to the layman without mentioning the word chance just why the nation's wage-structure takes the form it does.

It's a damned complicated business, Mike. I've been looking at their preliminary report on wages in what we call the devotional field. Take nursing, for instance – a job that clearly requires unlimited devotion. Obviously the general principle here is to make the wages as low as possible to keep out undesirable elements who would otherwise pour into nursing just to make a fast buck. But now we come up against a snag. What about surgeons? Don't they need devotion? Does their high pay mean that all the operating-theatres in the country are full of undesirables just out for the cash?

Well, I can tell you Nwexie took evidence on the last point from the PRO of the British Surgeons' Association, and he assured them at first hand that in the case of surgeons high salaries and devotion are entirely compatible. So they had to amend the principle to read: 'The greater the devotion required for a job, the lower the wages – except where applicants are likely to have a standing conferred by class or education which would put them above sordid financial considerations.'

But what about schoolteachers? A lot of them have a university education – and their salaries are derisory. So Nwexie amended the end of the formula to read: '. . . above sordid financial considerations – unless the work involves contact with minors, who could be corrupted by the flaunting of great wealth'.

You'd have thought that covered just about every complexity wage-structure in the devotional field could possess. Far from it. What about bishops? Aren't they well paid? And don't they confirm children? So Nwexie had to go to work once again and add: '. . . corrupted by the flaunting of great wealth – save where the noxious effects of such flaunting are neutralised by suitably uplifting ecclesiastical surroundings'.

We're still not out of the wood, though. What about people in other devotional jobs, like advertising or public relations? What about all the advertisers who sell things to children? Am I supposed to go and conduct my 'Meths for Men' campaign, to get teenagers drinking methylated spirits, in church, just so that I can justify being paid more than five pounds a week? So they had to add something about either uplifting ecclesiastical surroundings or a beneficial effect on profits.

And so on, and so on, until they had a formula twelve pages long. It certainly brings a gleam of logic into what at first sight one might think was entirely illogical. Nwexie wanted to reduce it to a simpler formula for the benefit of the man in the street. Christopher turned down 'You get what you grab' as being against the public interest. So it looks as if Smoothe's First Law of the Diffusion of Income, as I've suggested calling it, is going to read: 'Wages are what they are.' Drink up, old boy.

Brought to book

The literary life, which I have largely managed to avoid for my forty years as a professional writer, finally caught up on me with a rush last Tuesday afternoon. At about two o'clock my publishers rang to tell me that my novel *Headlong* was on the Booker shortlist. At about three o'clock someone announcing himself as the Arts Correspondent of the *Guardian* rang to tell me that I had been accused of plagiarism.

I was shaken, I have to admit. But not entirely displeased. This is what happens to writers in serious departments of the literary world, such as the Booker shortlist. They get accused of things. They hurl the accusations back in their accusers' teeth. There are rows and fights, and people don't speak to each other. No one had ever bothered to accuse me of plagiarism before. I had got somewhere in life at last.

And it was all happening with such breathtaking speed. I had been elevated to the literary peerage at two, and disgraced at three. This really was life in the fast lane.

Even more astonishing was that the accusation apparently came from one of the Booker judges themselves. The Arts Correspondent of the *Guardian* said he had been talking to John Sutherland, he said, who had told him that my novel bore suspicious similarities to a story by Roald Dahl.

'In your novel,' he said, 'there is a picture being used as a soot-guard in a fireplace. Yes?' I couldn't deny it. 'Well,' he said, 'in this story by Dahl there is apparently a piece of

225

Chippendale up a chimney.'

Soot-guard in a fireplace – Chippendale up a chimney. It looked black, I had to admit – and not just the picture or the Chippendale, but the whole case against me. I did indeed recall a story by Dahl which featured a furniture-dealer buying some valuable piece of furniture, possibly by Chippendale, off an ignorant yokel, though I couldn't recall the item in question being up a chimney at any point.

'But the *soot*?' I queried keenly. 'Was the Chippendale stopping the *soot* coming down the chimney?' Because if I could show that this crucial element in my version was original, it occurred to me – if it turned out that Dahl's Chippendale was stopping, say, Father Christmas rather than soot from coming down the chimney – then I had a complete answer to the charge.

The Arts Correspondent of the *Guardian* said he would find out and call me back. When he did he reported that he had misunderstood what John Sutherland had told him. There was no Chippendale up a chimney. The Chippendale-up-the-chimney charge had been totally withdrawn by the prosecution. What was now alleged was some general similarity between my plot and Dahl's.

This was even more baffling than the Chippendale up the chimney. I could remember the outlines of Dahl's plot, even if not the exact location of the furniture. Dealer cunningly persuades yokel that the Chippendale is valueless except as firewood – yokel obligingly chops it up while the dealer fetches his van. In my novel dealer and yokel are replaced by art historian and landowner. Art historian keeps his identification of landowner's picture as a missing Bruegel to himself; same story so far, I have to confess. Landowner, however, far from chopping it up, either literally or figuratively, becomes interested in it, in spite of art historian's dissembling, and tries to work out its correct identification for himself.

226

I explained this to the Arts Correspondent of the *Guardian*. 'This is the Booker,' he said apologetically. 'You have to expect this kind of thing.' He went off to take further instruction. Half-an-hour later he was back on the line. 'Martin!' he greeted me, in what sounded like some excitement. *Martin*? We seemed to be getting into very deep water indeed. Martin is the art historian in my novel. The Arts Correspondent of the *Guardian* was trying to phone my *character* to ask him whether he had been plagiarised! But this is exactly the kind of thing that happens in the higher reaches of the literary life! Fact and fiction turn out to be in some profound sense inextricably intertwined!

And I thought, 'This Arts Correspondent is no fool. He knows that Martin is the narrator of the story. He has information suggesting that it was *Martin* with his fingers in the till!'

I explained that he had got the wrong number, and that I was not Martin but Michael – Martin's author, certainly, but not responsible for his torts, surely, since Martin was of age and of sound mind. I urged him to ring Martin direct.

But when I open the *Guardian* next morning, there are our pictures. Not Dahl's and Martin's, but Dahl's and mine. Our names, as they say, have now been linked in the press. You can see from the reflective expression on Dahl's face that he is busy thinking up an original plot. You can see from the sly expression on mine that I am busy stealing it.

The pictures are illustrating John Sutherland's column. In the text Sutherland retails the accusation as an example of the kind of ridiculous nonsense that is probably going to be confected about the Booker finalists. 'Perhaps,' he says, as if he might actually believe it himself, 'the story lodged forgotten, like some old Bruegel, in the attic of the novelist's mind.' Though it's just as likely, he agrees, that the resemblance is 'purely accidental'.

So there the case rests. It may be plagiarism; on the other hand it may not be. What John Sutherland is too modest to mention is my much clearer and even more blatant plagiarism of *him*. There are glaring similarities between my book and his own excellent biography of Mrs Humphry Ward. Mrs Ward lives in a large house; so does the landowner in my story. Mrs Ward's house is in the country; so is my landowner's! Mrs Ward had difficult relations with her son; *so does my landowner*! In fact he has difficult relations with *two* sons, which by my calculation makes him twice as plagiarised as if he'd only had one.

Martin has obviously been up to his tricks again.

As the headline on John Sutherland's column says, You Couldn't Make It Up.